To my mother

Acknowledgment for poems which have appeared previously is made to: *the Age, Aspect Magazine, The Australian, Australian Poetry 1973, Blacksmith, The Bulletin,* the *Catalogue of the 1978-79 Poets' Travelling Exhibition, Compass, Contempa, The Ear in a Wheatfield, Helix, Leatherjacket, Magic Sam, Makar, Meanjin, Nation Review, New Poetry* (formerly *Poetry Magazine), Overland, Poetry and Prose Broadsheet, Poetry Australia, Poet's Choice, Polar Bear, The Rigmarole of the Hours, Southerly, Southern Review, Stand* (U.K.), *Surfers Paradise,* and *The Sydney University Union Recorder.*

Michael William Hulse,
Köln, 10 November 1992

SELECTED POEMS

SELECTED

POEMS

JOHN TRANTER

Hale & Iremonger

Typeset, printed & bound by
Southwood Press Pty Limited
80–92 Chapel Street, Marrickville, NSW

For the publisher
Hale & Iremonger Pty Limited
GPO Box 2552, Sydney, NSW

National Library of Australia Catalogue Card no. and
ISBN 0 86806 028 3 (casebound)
ISBN 0 86806 029 1 (paperbound)

Published with the assistance of the Literature Board of the Australia Council.

The author gratefully acknowledges the assistance of the Literature Board of the Australia Council for writing Fellowships during the years 1974, 1978, 1979–80 and 1982.

CONTENTS

AUTHOR'S PREFACE

In the last dozen years I have published six books of poetry, most of which are now out of print or unobtainable. This selection includes most of the poems from my published work which I would like to see kept in print, and a handful of recent poems, arranged in approximate chronological order, though with some compromises. 'Rimbaud and the Modernist Heresy' was begun in the early 1970s and finished nearly a decade later, as was 'Waiting for Myself to Appear'. The sonnets selected from *Crying in Early Infancy* span a period of some six years, during which three other of my books were published. I have rearranged these mainly to clarify the outlines of certain subgroups among them, while keeping the original numerals; they have no other identifying titles.

My thanks are due to the many people who have encouraged me to write, and whose friendship means a great deal to me. I cannot list them all on this page, and I trust they will excuse my not doing so. I owe particular thanks to the members of the Literature Board of the Australia Council, whose assistance made so much of my writing possible; to John A. Scott, for helping with this selection and many individual poems in it; and to my wife Lyn, who has given me constant support and encouragement.

THE MOMENT OF WAKING

She remarks how the style of a whole age
disappears into your gaze, at the moment
of waking. How sad you are
with your red shirt, your features
reminiscent of marble, your fabulous
boy-girl face like a sheet of mist
floating above a lake.

Someone hands me a ticket,
in Berlin a hunchback
is printing something hideous;
my passport is bruised with dark blue
and lilac inks. Morning again,
another room batters me awake
you will be haunting the mirror like silver . . .

now the nights punish me with dreams
of a harbour in Italy — you are there
hung in the sky on broken wings
as you always have been, dancing,
preparing to wound me with your
distant and terrible eyes.

THE PLANE

The plane drones low over Idaho,
a thundering shadow on the wheat.
The captain is thinking of a dust-cloud
disappearing out to sea.

The heavy wings tilt, a silo
looms abruptly. The cloud
falters on the horizon of his mind.
Taped to the cockpit wall is a photograph,
a piece of Sunday afternoon,
a lawn, a bright dress, flowers.
Soon they will be flying over the mountains
in a halo of ice. The cloud
hangs about, behind the imaginary trees.

WHITEY

At dawn, there was a knocking about
on the cold verandah, Whitey had come home
with both barrels hot to the touch.
The smell of cordite etched into his face.
Well, what a trip, what a journey.
The day's work done.

The next morning the view
from the verandah was an empty bite;
a stretch of cold grass led down to the trees.
Whitey was walking about down there
in the gloom of the trees like a pale
memory. Very intent
on a casual moving about,
both barrels cold as ice.
Well, what a morning, someone in the house
was making coffee.

THE CITY, THE TREE

1

The city allows the trees a little space
at the edges of the road that angles
somewhere out to the airport
and the open sky.

The trees wave and clatter,
warning us of something; the city
is busy, and when at rest
is better left alone.

2

This is the response the tree has
to the city: the film of lime
the skein of birds-feet, morning
polishing the blue windows of the 'Yacht Club'
where the tree reflects itself
in a thousand images of green.

THE NON-COMMERCIAL TRAVELLER

We found him down by the creek
crouched into the mud bank.
'Well, I'm lost . . .' as though
this foreign river was somewhere near town,
or the roadway up on the mountain.
He was locked up in a really neat
suit. His face shone
behind the white shirt. 'Say, phew . . .' Very odd,
David had to laugh. Nobody said much.

I noticed how easily we stood
on the bare earth. His shoes
seemed to puncture the ground.
'Well, I'm sorry,' he said, 'for all this.
I'm a commercial traveller. Lost my bag,
samples, whatever . . . don't bother looking.
Please go away.'
                                        We looked back from the ridge,
at the dull green foliage and the gleam of water.
There he goes, said David, into the river
laughing or crying, at this distance
difficult to tell.

THE WALL

you take in the shapes of the soft
flesh under the flare of sodium
the wet breast, the easy
buttock bunched with muscle, and the sly
twist on the polished floor.
your look is a razor.

waking is the antiseptic click
your face bleached in acid

    the fragments of the journey —
    the little girl walking away,
the burning horizon. the way the light
    descends onto your mouth. your laughter
    clutching at the night.

it is this vision which pursues me:
the 'ecstasy' behind the broken wall.

KABUL

From the broken, moving window
you see them alone in the desert afternoon
mad and burnt in a chorus of camels
walking somewhere invisible.

They have buried a city in the mountain.
A river like a soggy drain, they wash their feet
thinking of Tashkent gleaming out of Russia
across a plain of ice, the clack of a rifle bolt,
four thousand British corpses in the pass.
They dream their legacy of light
whatever the season.

HOW THEY SHOT THE SAVIOUR OF THE REPUBLIC

They locked him in a trunk and fed him
chemicals, he grew awkwardly
learning pain, and how to clutch
and prod clumsy features into grimaces
resembling *'green'* or *'mercy'*. How he escaped
they never knew, he crawled
miles under the bed of the Atlantic
feeding on mud, and dreaming
happy endings. The dawn found him
arising to radiant Brazil. Who knows,
they gave him the greeting he deserved.

THE ORANGE SPOT

The old drunk breaks into the midnight café,
begs a glass of water, reels into the welcome floor.

Later the 'Young Turk'
bearing a blade of malice in his back.

Why not lie together? having in common
a burnt-out bravery, equally sick of pushing out
the glare of life.

HOSPITAL

The pilot reaches for a drug:
like an insect he manipulates his way
through a jungle of bare furniture.
Footsteps approach. Receiving courage
he disperses into the air above Normandy.
A vapour-trail scribbles a quick signal

the key loosens the door
bringing methaqualone hydrochloride
and a wet smile. Drags him back
into the shrill traffic of the ordinary.

BALANCE

The traveller slouches at the table
handling the glass of pale sour liquid.
In the dim corner someone plays a mandolin
and the heat wavers at the door.

He can see the bus crawling away
into the desert. Having arrived nowhere, he finds
a portion of despair like a gun
settling into a comfortable balance in the hand.

BESTIARY

She haunts the bar in a loose, meandering fashion
imprinting glasses with lipstick and not caring.
Her mouth is bright and shoddy, having tasted
a 'little too much'. There are two paths of approach:

the youth hangs about in a grey cloud
of relative eagerness, biting the hand that admonishes.
Middle age flaunts the yellow stripe
of wisdom. The barman sees three animals
coiling in the imaginary grave.

THE ROAD BACK

A month ago he dropped out of his technicolor Belsen
with a bleeding head and a dry taste for 'life'.
Soaking out in a haze of suburbia, he keeps a softer drug
tugging at the nerve. Each night the cocaine freeway
blares at the back of his mind.

Now, calling on his old flame, the glow flickers into life
in a kind of mental soft-shoe and a shuffling laugh.
He lights up the kitchen in a vain attempt
to reconnect. 'Just passing through.'

He shoulders the black bag
clambers on the hog bike painted gold
blasts up the alley to the whistles of the factory boys
who know style when they see it and like to let you know
that where they breathe in the greasy gloom
the machinery wears a poisonous skin of rust
and the money's a hard grind.

He knows the money's hard to get.
He handles the hog with a pale strength
headed for the crowded highway and a busy trip.

ON THE TRACK OF THE ATTAINABLE

The ambitious minister from the smaller nation
outside the borders of history
through a lack of the will to be
makes up for flesh deficiency with another woman.
He has a bitter smell like a sick uncle that nobody wants
having good reason to drink failure.

Another night plunges into darkness
and symbols of alcohol and flame.
He drives across the city
from one flesh garret to another
gathering evidence of bones under the face
and articulated structures of pain.
He cries that he is ravished with the threat of death.
'My bones crack and tremble under the dirt!
My teeth mangling the worm!' Nightmare
made incarnate in every foul breath!

The larger nation affords an expansive smile
and wears golden ambassadors like a blessing
fingering out to Rio, Guadalcanal, Korea
fond in the delusion of money and the teeth of life.

MEMOIRS OF A FORTY-YEAR-OLD REVOLUTIONARY

I should say that I'm a wasted thirty-two
with a dropped womb and a taste for alcoholic failures.
But I am thirty-four, plenty of juice between my thighs,
and I have a young boy not at all alcoholic.

I know seven sophistries of revolution, practise none of them.
I do my best to be a tragic figure, but the boy laughs—
not even a whore in the cause, there are no whores here
in the red twilight. Not so much a worker

as a fellow traveller. I have a taste for leather jackets,
hard drink; my father beat me at the age of twelve.
I tell myself not to forget, but that's an old joke.
My wasted hatred filters to a logic of revenge.

The boy is mad on grass, that's his revolution.
Mine is to stay alive. Well, I've been to Laos,
Istanbul, left a trail of blood through Saragossa
that no one followed. The war is ended:

my damage is to stay alive. Perhaps I'm an amusing failure
perhaps I'm a woman, thirty-eight, a tiresome traveller
with a suitcase full of dumb disguises and a book
and phoney memories of Saragossa.

JULIE

So a witty vindictive inventiveness overtook them all;
Julie is dead. Her body smoulders,
releasing a sky full of rain, its own remedy.

Julie smiles, baits her tongue, waits at the end of the hall.
So a soft burning grows from her comedy;
red flesh on her shoulders: Julie is dead. That is all.

The shovel gathers some leaf on the drive—
gravel scatters from the claw. Jackdaw and brother
break summer's dream—Julie's alive
at foot of garden, bed of stream
somewhere in leaf-mulch and water.

So a damp cloud blots out the hill
and the track of a lewd pursuit—all to the good.
A sequence of notes to remember,
cipher clutched to the breast;
dishevelled memory, lack of repair due to a sudden thrill
that laid out Julie like a stroke of lightning and left the rest
wiping off a collective grin, fiddling with the dark hood
in the gloom of morning, the sky flushed red,
the sun flooding out a boon of benison. Julie is dead.

AT THE PICCOLO

Sitting in the jazz café at four a.m.
plotting a future in another country and a change of heart
I see a friend walk past with a striking woman
I happen to know has syphilis. His last girl was a lesbian
the one before that slit her wrist
four times in a week. Sitting at my table
with a Spanish coffee and a diary of despair
scribbling its lunatic message in my eyes
I think of two foreign girls with brutal inclinations
grappling on the gymnasium floor with their legs
awkwardly apart, smelling of stale perfume, honest toil
and a frank desire to please.

The girl thinks she might make the coffee
'on the house'. I'd back out of such a contract
on principle, remembering the advice of a friend
now married to a bitchy hag who used to be 'affectionate'.
Don't shit on your own doorstep, he said. Outside
the street takes on a pale radiance and a hint of mist.
My friend walks in, alone, and we talk
carefully avoiding references to women, love, despair
and the pale carnage of the street.

COUNTRY GIRL

You're a city man, I'm sure you like it
breaking open a new horizon for a girl like me;
but there's something nasty about the smile you take
when I begin to loosen. Can that be right?
Can you really be thrusting about under my dress
with your knotted hand? Oh man,
you've got something coming
you hardly know how to take. Take me,
you think I'm a simple bunch of juice,
I jump on the correct command, I'm just
oozing to do whatever you like; but baby
what you like had better be fucking good
and that's straight. Take a look

see yourself in twenty years, fingering a teenage bikie
in a gutter smelling of every colour of shit
with a nicer view hanging in a maple frame
in a room in your wrinkling head.

So soften up, take a tough reminder:
you're the kid who grew up loose in the streets
where the light was never expensive enough to see.
So now you've made the grade, you've made a waitress
with an understanding smile, a big heart,
and a lovely pair of tits. Big deal. Break off,

take a breather while you've got the time
and add up a few deposits on the side:
white, male, dishonoured by the print of death
and half-way down the slide.

SKETCH FOR A PORTRAIT OF A YOUNG WOMAN

Her desires cluster in a gathering of symptoms
like a new disease. She wears a certain colour
for complex reasons to do with the weather,
a feeling in the market, a tendency to anger
in the group she knows. Her hair is long, then short,
brown and gold, reflecting passion in a constant flux.
She wanders in the rooms where the talk
founders on the shelves of glass and liquid,
working out the early morning map of sense
with its ragged borders and shifting tides,
plotting out a fresh assault on love.

Her children froth and knock each other in the pool
drinking up the light with an easy greed
that beats against the glass. Yachts collide
in the windows' bright reflections, soft music
soaks into the corners. She frets, clutching her knuckles,
wondering if the new pain has gone awry, struck the target,
husband or lover; working at her life's tapestry
with an angular grace and a change of colour
for the new weather, for the latest mood,
for the hopeful market of repair.

WAITING FOR MYSELF TO APPEAR

1

Waiting for myself to appear
driving along a country road early in the morning
something unusual happens to my memories
as I trail the course of a sinister, mistaken river
where the perch hold convocation
of silence, cold, and dark . . .

Gliding into the suburbs
in a different pervasion of light: a blade of glass
quivers in the air, a sudden movement by the road,
a telephone jangling in my head . . .
somewhere in this brick and timber mess
there waits a shadow with manipulating hands,
already fondling a bottle
and a set of dark knives.

Cracking the speedo at a hundred plus,
adolescent, on a faster highway,
floating and sinking on the surface of the blurring tar
I caught myself dreaming of you
while the metal spat and scattered at the bushes.
How right that you should be waiting and not waiting,
busy with a schoolgirl honesty . . .
I guide the wheel with calm fingers
waiting for you to fall out of the future
with a laugh in your throat and a body
sick with love.

2

Years ago, locked up in a country school,
Flash Tony hardened his insolent mask
refusing to cut his hair, slicking up his boots,
burning out his lungs with nicotine
in a clumsy program of defiance.
Something of that hatred dragged you
into the school paddocks with him on an afternoon
miserable with rain. I have a glimpse of you
in a pink dress, climbing through a distant fence.

Next week we hitched a ride
with a truckie soft-headed on a hundred pills a day
to meet you in a country town. Tony fumbled around
buying you drinks, proud that you were twenty-three.
I was somewhere in the background like a faded image
taking it in, adding it all up.
There was a kind of taking
that was easy, a trade that was impossible.
'He is stupid, he is a boy,
but what can I do? How can I talk to you like this?
He is always drunk. What can I do?'

A year later you finally caught me on a midnight beach
getting over a bad case of youth.

3

When every gift of your damp lips is exhausted,
when the light has ceased to bathe your flesh
in sheets of white and gold, when the sea
has given you back the taste of your subtle skin,
when you have burnt out every reflex,
loosed my awkward limbs,
then you will become my harlot princess
in a kingdom of regret.

We can begin the heavy business of love,
burdened with memory and the manic need
to wipe clean the graph of nerves.

In my palace of isolation
when the night has touched your flesh
with motion and desire.

4

She tells me the track of a twisted
love, she sings to me
she claws the sweaty night: some new contraption
speeds to the horizon of her mind

and then explodes. When will you love me?
When will we marry?
I throw everything into your face!
My broken body! What will you say?

Fine, you've got all the ready money
and a fairly loose emotion for a friend
but if you think I'm frequent to acquire
better think again.

Back off, nothing's happening, you're through.
I've laughed like a freak, I've cried,
it's all over: boy you've got a long
history waiting to be tried.

Say you go further, in the hope of repair
or to make contact. So you think the links are in:
get your backing ready, make a deadline;
someone warm will pull the firing pin.

Well, she took it out, and did it badly:
he crawls around the wall experiencing heat;
down below in the drive-in morgue they're packing up
dead meat.

5

I am so pleased with you, she said,
for what you have done to me.
First of all, we had something to wait for;
you liked me to be strong in affection
and in the way I might light you up,
and you said to me 'turn it on'.

Bring me out of this dream, it's too much savagery;
I have a better place on the island, if you only knew,
where I have planned for our eventual future . . .

But something drew you into forgetfulness
and we faded out of touch. When is the joint meeting,
when can you make the connection? When can you
turn about, smiling . . . I want you to come around
treating the neighbours with a due respect
and plan the study, and the new design
incorporating an 'alcohol den' for the dispossessed.
There we could tame our grief, if you would wish . . .

Something obscure trouble you? Something a little touchy?
Take a relief, it's me, fondling my way
into your cold arms again and again:
for all you're worth, it's a new explosion,
and I would be glad to welcome your approach.

Is anything the truth? And is it easy? You've troubled me
half ready to bleed to death for my sake, although
God knows, it's only a game, and far too late for that.
Well, whenever you're ready
we'll take off our clothing and give one another
a damn good appraisal. We both suffer something
invisible; and you, having broken into the sky . . .

6 *(for George Alexandrov)*

He slipped the needle through the vein
and tried again. 'Blood. Too much blood,
it's enough to make you sick.' As he said to me
one night full of rain, take this coke,
it's nothing, he said, this coke
is well under control. We both laughed
at the joke, and I went away. 'I keep bleeding like a pig,
I can't hold myself under control any more,
but the coke's all right.' I laughed again,
as I had five years ago when he was all right.
His brother died on the floor of a deserted room.
She was alone in the carriage. She left herself on the train
past her destination till the end of the line
in the far country under the cold layer of cloud.

7 *(Herat — Kandehar, 1967)*

Distance is not the mountain on the rim
shifting in the glass of a cheap drug
nor the net of babble in the night bus
but a sickness in the sun always rising
into heat above an unfamiliar landscape.
As sleep turns luminescent, a jungle
tilts up out of the sea. Nothing is easy,
nothing is what you imagine in the blue trip,
nothing familiar, but the moon over Kandehar
in the desert morning, and the morning star,
as the town comes up at you in sudden release . . .

He went away for a long time.
At great expense of strength he found a desert.
He is only a young man; the remedy
is almost elegant: Librium, tetrahydrocannabinol.
A soft trip, he makes
the hard-worked anodyne a path to reverie.

More painful is the distance and the ceaseless movement,
as he hopes to return. Most of his friends are dead.

8

I can see your limbs gleaming on the carpet
in the half-lit room, the sweet tobacco scent,
how the scatter of punctures on your arm
plotted out the vein;

I brought flasks of sharp dry liquor
that stripped layers from your skin
exposing all the young girls in your breast.
You would soak the light into your flesh

so the glow of your body would give eloquence
to the night, that now stammers in a neon fit of gloom . . .
but that was in another country, and now you are always
here, and just out of reach . . . middle age

growing like a slum around your future.
You are a ghost, watching over my shoulder
as I start to grow old. It is late at night.
I am waiting for myself to appear.

CONVERSATIONS

In the house of poetry nothing remains except
that which was written with blood to be listened to with blood.
Pablo Neruda

1

'On the rack of the long expected I take back
and electrify . . . a fatal disease,' claims Cronstadt,
middle-aged, the drunk poet in the park. 'The Poet
lobs a verbal hand-grenade. The drug explodes, a hot
poppy in the willing flesh.' He is on his knees
scrabbling for his 'Poems'. His fingers
accidentally trigger off a gust of memory.
'It's no good talking about Greek legends
to me! I have an obstinate devotion to life
as it is lived . . . I have lived here in the park
through a hundred morbid cycles, the crisis and the loss,
watching the brutal forces eating their way
into the features of old men, sluts, children
fucking in the leafy dark, a landscape built
with dust and vomit. Talk to me of money wasted,
leprosy, how the wine turns bitter in the glass,
but don't bring your book-learning here
and talk about the "spirit of decay".'
So he limps from brothel to asylum
trailing a thin steel shaft, plotting
ruinous conjunctions. Later,
when his latest needle blots out time,
he is up to his bowels in black mud
digging at the roots of the city;
at such a depth of filth can only pray
for the simplest miracles: breath,
coolness, and a rising sun.

2

'My new experiment, to be heroic.'
Cronstadt can amuse himself with pain,
washing out his guts with poison. On the screen
the automatic rifles' rattling burst
chopped a death salad through the leaves.
Cronstadt approved his own disgust. 'Better to corrupt
nature with each verbal stroke; so does art
destroy life in a frenzy of bad images.'
His new harlot sucks another chocolate mint, confiding:
'Roses, he brought me, something gained . . .'
more than mutilated feelings. 'The brute!' She lies
that she is hurt, or bad, or wounded.
'Cheeky bitch! Cheek! Cheek!' Her little girl flinched
back, curled on the blanket, weeping at the window
and the rain river sheathing the glass.
I grant him this: he knows the slaughterhouse,
bright scarlet brook of horror, how the red
darkens to amethyst and maroon
and how the flushed and drunken moon drags the truth
from a city, from the bleeding sex,
and how to trade such knowledge to advantage.
Nothing less than the emotions' bribery
and rank corruption of experience would wrench a girl
to such grovelling, white skin and bone
bathed in the television flash and glow
that freezes all that you observe, leaking forth
as the Poem.

3

'Approach the Poem with no less care than you would
a dangerous companion,' was his last remark
as evening sifted down onto the conversation pit.
'A whole career ended,' he would say,
'as though nightmare flickered into light,' as the Poem
sagged into itself
'Sweeping up this trash . . .' wreckage,
pentameters crushed against the Verb
'More pollution! As though . . . night . . .'
as though a harsh collections of mouthings
transcended the spittle, the hackneyed breath, trash
from three continents, to burst into the real!
You know the lash of something else, Cronstadt, and
how to utilise the new trick, confessing pain . . .
you, touching a nerve, moving closer
black with hate and money, foul with love.
'Somebody has to lose out,' he suggested,
buying up a much-abused virginity
she who would offer no resistance to a gainful trade—
naked willingly, a lover stripped of metaphors—
underwriting only the regret, and that later,
when Cronstadt's craving for a kill had been appeased
in his own transparent way: 'Take a desire, my boy,
and *appease* it!' So he would flay
the remnants of his ill-fitting life
prepared at the morning window washed with light—
the whip, the grin, the teeth, the monkey suit.

4

'More news from the front,' whispered a friend,
wiping the message with a finger in a melting line
across the frosted glass. Cronstadt returns
from the evening assay of concern.
'Few of my suckers left,' a weak smile, 'few
to sip the nectar.' Later, plied with drink
he may condescend to lift the fog
from a scene glowing with cold phosphorus
to reveal the corpse, a friendship
and a lust for meaning. The broken body
much abused in its energy
becomes the new syntax, the new
hairshirt in a lusty weave. The Poem.
'I load the glass with three conceptions,
enough for life. To see, to pluck the rot
and set it growing in a bowl, to explicate. Drink.
The drinks are free.' The glass slopped over with a rag,
the line dissolves into a vista of the street:
some hunched monster approaches in shreds,
claws at the pane that lately held the Poem
in a flux of molten quartz. *'Mon semblable! Pitoyable frère!*
Make him dance, and beg, and give him wine! The hero thus
distils himself . . .' But he has pushed the metaphor too far.
The monster breaks the window with a clumsy blow
confronting Cronstadt with a double image of defeat:
the message buried in a heap of shattered glass
and a slab of wet light on the pavement of an empty street.

5

Taking the air along the boulevard, he airs his view:
to make a poem, an act of suicide; to love a woman, worse;
and 'Give up life, my boy, there's nothing in it!'
He's growing old. He stops to have a drink. The alcohol
inflames him to regret. 'So many bitches! And yet, the clay
creates the Work!' Across the road, behind the sunset
in a window, a naked woman saunters through a room.
Down in the street a sports car mutters at the lights.
The city stops. Cronstadt drowns
in the glass, in the rivers of flesh. 'My mind heats up—
over there, the city smoulders on the rim. Red neon
burning in the rain. Night extends its needles
through the brain. And you? When will you prepare yourself
to welcome failure? Your feeble style, emotion's
haberdashery, wasted entertainment, a naive
balance to the good. You claim I dwell too much
on the obscene. It's a way of pitying the suffering mass,'
he would profess, breaking his face across the intersections
in the complex mirror. 'Some way of making up a debt.'
And then another drink, and later, weeping: with a dirty rag
he'd wipe his sopping face and try to laugh.
'Many times I have approached the real,
and pushed too hard.' Now it seems at last that he is sickened
with his own destruction. 'My boy, take a good look at me
and see what thirty years of bright living have done:
I've got all the music taped, and a burnt-out freedom,
and no more ammunition in the gun.'

RED MOVIE

That which can be studied is the pattern of processes which characterise the interaction of personalities in particular recurrent situations or fields which 'include' the observer.
Harry S. Sullivan, in *Tensions That Cause War*

1. *The New Field of Knowledge*

when the new alphabet soup of the earth
is raised into a flag, the inevitable wind appears
with its own 'sister to breath'.
the streamers appeared, he grew forward,
as though a new field of knowledge
drew breath, promised itself

a blue field will always invade you.
here, you can become a little more
becoming: the streaming sister,
enveloped in a flag of brutality, draws a ration
of sense, bleeds rationality . . .

a willow's image follows me into the dark
a delicate cowboy, so blue, his dawn
sky
is
too.

⋆

we breathe like fish in this
glass-tinted gloom.   the music room.
plugged in.   headphones.   out there

the grass deepens from a washed-out yellow
to a solemn green.

we drift across the lawn.

standing at the entrance
to a cold landscape filled with rain
firing into the trees, the gun
bucking against your heart.

London.   5 a.m.   summer.
the sodden corpse of a monkey
floating on the oiled canal.

evening.   the woman crouches in the flare
reflected from the new ocean.

thoughts of silver oppress the lake
                              :such light

opening a way through . . .
                              I'm thinking

2. *Extract from the Ice Diary*

he apologised for the delay
owing to illness
one accurate acknowledgment of the place of dirt
one brief flirtation with 'owing to illness'
a couple
of reparations, cancelling the attainment

I will always want something like you

*

a man settles onto the earth
pursuing a small rodent in a dreamy light
hoping for 'escape'

a man repairs his only dream with blunt fingers
unused to despair's tasselation, how he unravels
the structure of the small animal
'in the hope of discovering an opening!'

★

the creek bleeds with a little blue

we see the pieces of the dream

carefully arranged, but lacking a certain touch
the pressure, the requisite alchemy

so the cloud, the rain
complete the picture
almost to perfection   the creek

a dreaming flag billows out
a wet stripe of green

★

an experiment which succeeds, he said,
wiping the breath from his face
which had started to congeal
is no longer an experiment, but has become
a demonstration of the obvious.

this said, as he struck out at the images
gathered on the mountain
to drench him with the gust of life.

★

hunger developed a bitter attitude.
we were more deprived
as the night grew, finally filling the sky.

one thing I prophesy: light will spread
from the other rim of cloud, and bring a season.
treat it well

★

a desert, this appalling gaze
allow it to pervade the skin
that encapsulates a bitter taste of blue
proffer the blade
in the hope of an eloquent movement

forgive her face
for what it cannot conceal
offer something without hope
of a receptive 'attitude'

I will always invade you

prepared to ascend the stair
loosen up, become aggressive
let her warm you up
if that becomes a problem

départ! départ!

'ma faim'

★

the poem will allow you to move.   a girl is burning
in her underwear.   leaving this continuum in rags
shattered desert . . . he can allow me to travel
from this insight:

stopped the track.   if this trick
I will allow you to depart

'if it's all you want'; how piteous, such a mistake
brings back a river of what you can least afford
in your present extremity: God bless you

in your present grasp
of an unidentified illusion

as if resisting a new stripe of colours
a whole street . . . I'm thinking . . .
in a new suit of hands
                                        . . . as though fallen
from a shelf of ice, newly frightened,
he prepared the scent of mint for the roadway

a new cloud appeared.   a helicopter chopped its way
through the blue
his blades
are
too

★

the small man polished up the regiment:
they stood about on dawn parade.
the sun drifted through the mist behind the trees.

across the gravel road, in the bushes
were some bona fide travellers, also
skulking.   something else happened.   to the poem

★

an experiment which has failed is no longer
an experiment.   it is, he smiled,
nothing more promising than a failure.

★

listen to me: you're enjoying nothing
seen from this crisp angle

listen to me: I have been travelling for some time
aware of the necessity for choice: move!
if you wish to unravel the sources of your own sorrow
if you wish to divert the river of absolution
if you are desperate for a chance
to break up

choose the song most suited
to your movements, to your fatal
and impossible beauty

summer's tattered flag your winding sheet
fate's tackle and gear
drops you by the neck

whatever song you bring
to the country of hope

3. *The Death Circus*

the death circus moves in.
all you're worth is in it
the man with the plastic face
opens up his graves for you to see

the lady with the soft legs
opens up in the night
all the moon
long, the bitter light
chews at our faces.   you will not like
the happy flame circus in the roaring dark

we were taking a ride
way out south, somewhere you have never been
into a country of cold beauty
the salamander circus
followed like a hungry dog

4. *The Failure of Sentiment and the Evasion of Love*

morning hunches like a gathering of men
in damp overcoats, waiting for something to happen

shudders into light: the death transfusion breaks
some news: confusion of tongues

flesh in the oral cavity! slips
across the lip as the big dude
breaks down: sack of slack meat on the flash divan

broke up and cried like a baby.
you'll help me pick up the pieces,
won't you, my prince of light . . .
won't you, won't you,

*

she disheartens into a dirty bed
huddling a knoll of pleasure to herself.

the light goes peachy.   something
trundles out of the forest.   morning
edges a little nearer.

he investigates the hospital where her mind
will have to be repaired.   nothing he could do
would warm the ravenous flesh,
none of his movements
blunt the starved edge.

he thinks he is ready to go somewhere
but the gasoline reeks out of the tank
blood runs from the fingers like red ink
from a leaking pen.

now the girl stands in the concrete yard.
her eyes go white, reflecting
the sky she has come to love,
that has so little of the human in it.

her look turns back against her with a jealousy
beyond repair.

*

he said: I could have moved, but
only to wound.   unlock
the gentle embrace.   like water.

much later, the return:
his sight broken,
drowned, his face
soft as water.

whenever he altered his appearance she would cry
he became less concerned

how do you know I have loved you?
why do you return?   is it my flesh?   you want?
to touch?   why do you inflict yourself?
how am I guilty?   who is it,
in the shadow of the forest?

'ce n'est rien: j'y suis, j'y suis toujours . . .'

*

there is something about flesh
which defeats me.   or hair
flowing into light.   you
you know these movements,
you with your 'big smile'.
come here, bring me the liquid
left overnight to breed
'big dreams'. I hear the blind man's tap
tapping at the pane.   he brings his own music.

as your body moves in the glass, your hands
wound me.   thus.   moving.   such
music, music, music; the mind
preparing the re-entry program
controls the tiny movements of air.

you say this music
has the power to maim;
I know such a gesturing of flesh wavers
on the border of its own reflection.   movement.
love.   the wall of noise.

*

I am leaving in the morning, says the
young husband of a few days.   yes.
break my heart if that's what you want.   that's not
what I want.   bring me the coffee.
cold again.   why I love you

look at you, you're crying, shit you're a nasty
coward, to hurt me.   like this.
look at your eye, blowing up,
filled with water.

*

your breast is very round, if such
geometry were possible.   juice,
of a sort, is promised.   he says
let me alone, he says *bitch teeth*

later they are alone
with an animal for company they call
cat, or the night
trembles into neon, or the morning
hurts over the sleeping city, crying
breast, breast,

⋆

he throws away the glass
prepared to be damaged

he makes machinery of his arms
that were accustomed to giving

a black hood protects him
from Nothing

a shout from the street
breaks red into his vision:
he desires something like himself

⋆

shaving, the razor warps in the glass
and slides beneath a rusty green film.
behind his shoulder, a window
choked with white.   she
slouches at the end of the hall, an angry girl
gaping at the bright windy hill and the sun
washing the street.   *youth breaking into age*
corrupts reflections of itself

when I sleep lately it's a black kingdom
pulls me under like a tide

Khan coming out of Mongolia—
changes from the outside,
Egyptian traits . . .

the question that inevitably comes.

5. *The Knowledge of Our Buried Life*

the dreadful sailor fills the dark
with his strange descant, building

sepulchres of ruin in the past.
to make him go, the dumb tongue

wallows in the mouth.   in the courtyard
rain flares on the cobbles

the fountain flails the rocky lip
and will not cease.   he reaches an exhausted sleep

late at night, and dreaming of Asia.
darkness resumes the tables, and the sailor

filled with night and the ocean, departed
as one leaves a sleeping port

at dawn, the water gleaming from below
and the harbour silent.

★

improbable alterations overtake the coolest nightmare:
though each is a clear flag of the dreamer
it turns up the soil in his own field like a stranger.

the struggle of objects against their fate
is not cancelled: the field fluctuates as the act of seeing
imprints the world with the reflections of a colder dream.

*

the fog grows from the harbour's leaden mirror
discovered by a pale dawn

correcting the village's advance
into day. *aube*, he said, *aubade*

at a faint distance someone cried a noun
as some presence awoke from the steep hill

and moved down to the sea which was crying
in the voice of gulls

aubade

aubade

*

I would like you to unwrap the mood
most suited to your present grasp
as though you could control the desire
of your own wasteful preparation

I think we are in winter again
if you are ready
we can begin

MARK

Mark finished it himself, choosing midnight
and a garbage-littered swamp. He scrawled a note
and stuffed it in a pocket: 'Like shooting a dog.
The Vibrations. Someone please try to bring me back.'
They pulled him from the mud and dressed him up
and put him underground again. A week before that
he'd grabbed me in the street, shaking,
speaking in a foreign tongue. Lost for seven years.
'It's all right, I'll move along,' he said. Cosmic radiation
fried his brain. He had tapped a private source
of horror clichés; nightmare rushed out,
and the gestures that he used in self-defence
were worn threadbare with too much fingering.
He wove a plot to save the masses; loners,
misbegotten, drifting on the edges of Night City.
All he needed was 'charisma'. One day he left a note:
'The Princess: She must be saved, even at the cost of death,
her own death, if need be. I'm sorry that I cut the Cross
against the grain, damaging the door. Yours. Mark.'
Vibrations called him from a network
on the other side of town. He had scuttled off
by the time the medics came to strap him down.

Once, years ago, when he was 'elegant', he brought us wine;
we ate well, and drank by candlelight. It seemed that sanity
was easily bought; one needed only to be young.
Methedrine, in moderation, kept him on the track.
'I'm not interested,' the doctor said, 'in arty reminiscences.
Find the stupid prick and bring him back.'

THE GUADALCANAL MOTEL

They hold no holidays at the Guadalcanal Motel;
the Sergeant stumps about the dusty yard
trying out his new leg and the President weeps
in his spider-web study, while the peons
run chattering off the rocks and drown themselves
in the grey Pacific. They make no mourning,
keeping part of their trivial sorrow in reserve
for the day when it will be needed again,
for the night when the blue troops splash ashore
and rake the sandhills into patchwork ratshit,
bringing the Guadalcanal Motel into the arms
of the New Republic amid a litter of spent shells.
They haunt the American conscience like a rotten nightmare
in a flicker of old movie clips: 'Platoon Five!
Take the hill!' And the ambulance drivers
weep and slash the air with glass slivers
from a shattered windscreen. They take no leave,
beating the stubborn earth with blunt clubs
in a travesty of agriculture, and ripping up
whatever foliage they might encounter, which is not much,
green being a surreal and worthless luxury
in the Motel trenches. Each morning they salute the statues

of the ancient king who sold them into slavery
and the franchise king who brought them
money, poverty and Coca Cola.

GUERNICA

There's no use questioning the wretch
with his face in tatters and the bandolier
holding his guts together. You'd be better
stretching on the cobblestones beneath a tank
to get a view: that tank across the village square
aiming its throat at the running grenadier
and the hog-leg pistol in his belt.
Take the Stuka staking out the air
with banshee breath; the bombing pilot
has a dark complexion, and his thumb on the button
is very easily dealing death. There is no
postcard view of the town, in this ruin,
though russet palms flock to the 'Med'
as they have donc before, and delighted many.
Take the army, in its various wreck,
and the rising tide of dead, who cry to us
through the watery lens: Huh! You!
Tomorrow we are mutton! Any nightmare
is equal when the dream chokes to an end!
If you like the beach you'll find the water blue.
The blasting Oerlikon executes a rhyme
and strips the pilot from his sight.

There's no use cornering the gunner in his grief.
His fingers rest along the rim of night.

THE DISADVANTAGE OF THE DIESEL ENGINE

On or about the time of the death of your friend, did you make certain inflammatory remarks to the effect that the promulgation of a state of bliss (*Ananda*) was both the responsibility of the State and the inalienable right of the Working Class?
— No.
Did you attempt to convince certain members of the USAID mission at Loc Nol that this state of bliss (*Ananda*) could be likened metaphorically to that state of mechanical repose evidenced by the U-Boat of the 'Tiger' class under the command of a distant relative of Field-Marshal Rommel at about 0530 hours on the 29th of April, 1943?
— Yes.
Was this state of knowledge-being-awareness (*Sat-Chit-Ananda*) reported missing in action during the closing phases of the Pacific war?
— Yes.

How did you describe the advantages of this gambit?
— The U-Boat was resting on the surface of the water.
What was the reason given for this action?
— Brahman was charging its batteries.

THE RISE AND FALL OF THE THIRD REICH

On or about the time of the funeral of your friend, did you make certain remarks referring to the hypothesised connection between the 'desire' of Brahman to perceive itself, and the projected re-emergence of the NSDAP?
— It's possible. I think I was either 'stoned' or 'being stoned' at the time.
You were observed in conversation with a 'young woman'. Is this 'woman' a 'friend'?
— No.
Did you later describe this woman as a 'good screw'?
— No. (Aircraft noise)
Do you wish to continue this conversation?
— Conversation?

Do you wish to avoid these questions which, spreading their roots, bring in the end only *ivresse et folie*?
— Ah-*oo*-gah! Ah-*oo*-gah!
Are you about to dive?
— Yes.
Is it true that I am mentally unstable?

POEM ENDING WITH A LINE BY RIMBAUD

He: It is easier to like the soldier
when he laughs and shoots a foaming dog
rather than a man, or child, and easier then
to hold the hand grenade. No plane comes
down faster when the jets are shot
than the law of gravity allows. Let the radar
plot, let the men drink poisoned lemonade.
It is better to allow the tide
to bring the fish in as they will,
or in that shoal as that shoal moves
like a flock of leaves across the hill,
across the traffic and the school of windscreens
damp with love. Leave the office,
leash the dog that nibbles at his bone,
bring all your country longings to an end.
Prepare your face to be an imprint of the scene—
the clock, the limping man, the cash machine.
Wax the ski. Compress the snow.

She: *Et mon bureau?*

CHEAP THRILLS

One error, in fact, of eccentricity in poetry is to seek for new human emotions to express; and in this search for novelty in the wrong place it discovers the perverse.
T. S. Eliot

WHAT CAMUS SAID

Peta, flayed red on the harrowed sand.
Dune buggy aerials across the tattered sky.
'I dropped surfing,' she said, 'you know,
too slow, all that bullshit mysticism.
Give me a good stretch of tar,
something to break the monotony.
What was it Camus said? He bought his
in an auto wreck. He should know.
Want a steak?' Nothing more personal
than the firm muscle, sheen of sweat;
she tricked you with a sly honesty.
'I suppose you'd say it's sexual,
I mean, that gearstick stuff.'

I watched her drop back into second
just before the crest. She
shot off the top of the sand ridge
and vanished: Camus, Frank O'Hara,
all the restless ghosts.

LOVE STORY

They had lunch by the lake
then they gathered up their movements and drove
head first into the accident of the city.
Will you move into my apartment?
Will you climb out of bed at sunrise?
They drove out into the country of trees.
I would like the season to be grateful
in the way it has of being less than cruel.
Showers, easy traffic, make up the symphony
they wallow in, in the framework of personal
past tense, now that we watch them
flashed and faded in the photograph.
They sat behind the window of the limousine
and watched the sun rise into the weather.

They drove head first
into the beautiful accident.

THE BIG PORSCHE

We watched Sebring on a crate of beer,
the sick men in the mad machinery.
Pushing two hundred past the flag.
'Take that McQueen — can he *drive*!
And with a broken foot!'
She swung the spanner, clank!
clank! against the block. 'No cracks
there, at any rate. See you at Monaco.'

She wrapped it up later, the big Porsche,
and they had to pull her out of the wreck.
Six months in hospital, and she said to me
'Well, he came in second, but he was
wheeling it on his own. Did you
see the interview? He looked awful.
Christ it hurt.'

THE TERRITORY OF DARKNESS

Under the pressure of great acceleration
the heavy cars left the grid. Hours later
there were no vehicles to be seen.
We visited Italy on an impulse, she said. Two cars
fled around the corner. One red, one green.
The sky was a terrible white.
They were 'in pursuit of speed'.
We left the country late that evening under cover
of high velocity, thunder from a twin exhaust
and low cloud. There were flowers at the border
for the drivers of the cars which had vanished
into the territory of darkness. One of the borders
turned red in the night.

The air was obsessive, the cars followed
at incredible speed, into the darkness.
The next time we returned under cover
of a dubious cargo, drifting through the mist at dawn,
there were no drivers to be seen.

THE DUBIOUS SYNTHESIS

Peta made it easy for the boy: good food,
a dab of poetry, a lust for dictionaries.
She was amusing, all right, moving fast
to keep the mistakes under control.
'How difficult,' she complained to me once,
'how tiresome to wear a whole society like a pack!
The weight! the stupidities! the greed!'
Nonetheless she made a job of it. She
made it difficult for all of them: bad faith,
a stab at honesty, abusive literacy.
'How simple it would be,' she told me,
'to shuck off the whole greedy pack. Friends,
lovers. Chuck the lot of them!'

'I keep making some synthesis,' she said,
'and it never works. Speed, power, greed.
Do you call this living?'

COMPROMISE

Certain vehicles are produced for luxury.
The engineer removes his overcoat
and steps into the spartan frame. Steel surrounds him,
fittingly. He moves the vehicle at great speed
along the motorway. The girl in the skimpy mink
climbs into the leather seat and rushes about
in a frenzy of comfort. She would like more speed!
Other vehicles have the aim of brutal power.
The staff of the engineer are all regretful,
attempting to steer a middle course.
They come together in a new design:
staff, engineer, the girl who gets around.
They move about the highways in a game of elegance
dreaming of metal, markets, power, contradictions.

The people of the countryside also move about,
strapped to the spartan frame of compromise.

MAKING IT

He idles home along the waterfront at dawn,
the motor ticking over. The sun is an orange blob
on a lake of blue paint, he thinks.
He is not often wrong. Peta languishes in her apartment
as well as she can, which is easily
though lacking style. The sun gives a bright shudder
across the mirror in the marble room.
It is all because of the money! she imagines.
She is wrong. He is a big hairy bastard! The money!
He has another girl in Switzerland,
another car, another bank account.
The red Daytona ticks along as best it can,
which is very well indeed. He thinks:
She is *wham*! *Big tits*! He is an American.
She thinks: wham! big tits! so what,
desiring the pretty chambermaid. She is sometimes
so inclined: wham! motor car! chambermaid!

The sun does its best to rise over the Mediterranean
and make a big blue day. They love, as best they can,
which is very clumsily, but well.

MONEY IS A KIND OF POETRY

Consider the images which orbit
around the red Ferrari: style, expertise,
aggression. Consider the manipulation
of the symbols which surround the red Ferrari,
consider the bull in the ring, how the colours
bring him to madness. If it is possible
the machine will excite certain glands,
if it can be done the car will break up
under the strain. There is much to be considered:
engineering subtlety, brutality, immense
advertising. Consider the money

that whirls in a heated constellation
in the vast brain of the red Ferrari.

THE QUESTION OF VALUES

It was too late to leave for France, with the snow
embroidering the brown sky. There was a rime of dirty ice
along the edges of the gravel, and sour green
where rotting leaves splashed the lawn.
'So we stayed with the countess,' said Peta, 'though
we knew she wasn't real.' Two lightning flashes laced
the uniform she wore. It was predictable:
history repeating itself across the lake, justice
perverted to a cruel luxury. The dark came early,
moved down from the alps in a silent avalanche
and filled the grounds. So they lived, for an afternoon,
in an 'atmosphere of monstrous corruption'.
She would talk about it later as a watershed,
a time of sickness when the will became infected
and led the spirit to stumble through the future
with a repetitive spasm. 'You know I look sane,'
she said, 'and beautiful; but by God
you don't know the half of what I lost.
When things are possible, their value, good or bad,
can come to less than nothing. Is that right?'

It was too late to leave for Paris. Vast hail
slaked the damp grey countryside. 'We were very
young,' said Peta. 'It would seem.'

THE LAST RUN

Coming over the pass in poor weather —
Peta at the wheel — into a new countryside
and a different view of hard labour.
There was time enough to taste an apprenticeship
to cheap thrills, but a loose one in the group
brought bad news — some train wreck,
a touchy omen of sex developed to hysteria.
We left the most expendable friendships at the station.
Disaster gambled for our favour, Doctor Threat
made a subtle play for our regard. No chance, with such a
tight judiciary, so we filled the tank and moved out.
The weather querulous, all the roads bad
and a troubled motor — these deterred,
though soft hands were capable.
'Did I tell you about Paolo? And the Dwarf Intelligence?'
Something to do with the police in another state,
another frame of mind. So we told stories,
mostly true, about the taste of youth for foolishness
and high speed. Darkness moved on.

We were soon out of danger and through the pass —
the last run, she promised,
though we knew it wouldn't keep.
Too much truth in sex, too much opportunity
for soft developments. Looking back
over the mountains where the frost
bit our shoes, she said 'Damn it,
I liked the countryside,
and the people who escaped.'

THE DISTILLATION OF A STYLE

They were running well ahead of time
when a jagged flash cracked the perspex
and the road skidded out of sight.
A fighter plane drops over the rise
and leaps forward for the sea. I am left
to think on eagerness. They were willing
to leave risk out of the reckoning so that a style
could be distilled: trim, essential, tight,
without encumbrances and no remorse,
lopping off a second from the reflex arc.
They broke through the forest and down the slope
with a burst of power. Some detail bent askew.
They tracked a red splash along a wall
and left a smudge of oilsmoke wiped across the sky
in a hasty scrawl, an empty valley,

and a fighter plane dwindling into the cloudbank
where the line of sea attempts a perfect emptiness.

THE SUMMING-UP

Some time later I visited the scene of devastation.
The tyre marks were still there, held in reverence
by those whose bitterness had tied them down
and whose accommodation to a new political reality
had bought them cheap. The press was active, it was said,
papers fluttered through the cafés, fat fingers
fiddled with a dozen rings. The girl
was raddled with the need to kill:
'Peta and the needle — tell me,
how do *you* deal with such memory?'
As the women moved among the tables
in a morbid shoal, the light appeared to fail.
I remembered Peta at the crossroads braking hard
in a dangerous shift that quickly gained acceptance,
admirers, a slow disintegration into decadence.
The smart boys are dressed up, moving out,
and what was oncc uniquc, a gcsturc, risk
that stung with beauty, has now become a cheapened ritual.

How is it that such things pass from guesswork imitation
into wonder — that much is easy — then to dance,
animal dance beneath the trees? How is it
that the café crowd applauds a riddle,
when the key — Peta was beautiful, in a phrase —
would turn their flattery to hate?
How is it that pain will hunt so far,
and such a victim?

THE POEM IN LOVE

It's possible that a poem in its own realm of being may take on
a life of its own, and thus return by means of love some of the anguish
and the suffering invested by the poet in its creation.
Paul Ducasse

1

There's no end to this thing, it moves out,
killing. Difficult to find, yet it lives on
in plain daylight free of detectives
avoiding the plastic explosives. Like the
Gatling gun it clacks around in a windmill comedy
of noise and portability (you never know
when you might need to love it again,
and thus you'll have to carry it about, won't you)

or, later, in the French café of its choice, quite
independent of you (and yet you thought of it,
didn't you, or gave it life, or
something similar free of plastic
mint alcohol, in its own amusement
to its own delight

2

Then it moves on, and you are heartstruck
or stagebroken, but later you will ride out
dressed in black, on a moon-blue palomino
of your own choosing to match the scenery
and find it hiding somewhere again! and you
will laugh, possibly, and grip its hand
and take it to the beach of its richest liking
and if you will find driftwood and light the fire

put on some coffee and the aromatics of its choice,
perhaps it may promise never to leave you again!
And you will laugh at this foolish 'promise'!
knowing (having made the creature) how it misbehaves
understandably, having to avoid the trap of aromatics,
burnt coffee, and a million tons of love.

3

'Free at last!' you will smile, self-deluded,
knowing your tears ready to gush at the slightest
memory of its beauty, and all the dumb remembrances
dogging your darkness when you sleep alone
and dream of catching it again and how you will hold
hands et cetera in a foam bath of love!
You sleep alone with staring eyes and
a handful of mint leaves tousled in your hair

(your freshly washed hair, beautiful!) and you are still
hoping to stun it again, and have it all,
all for yourself like a schoolgirl . . . you,
fool, stagestruck clubfinger, still in love
with its aroma, with its sweet dreams aroma
bullshit nerve gas platitudes!

4

Sunstruck on Wilshire Boulevard nothing makes sense,
autos starved of gas and people drivelling,
and yet . . . yet you remember Coleridge, and several
Revolutions! How do you explain it? With the
tears running down like that? Your makeup
blown and your cover shredded up? You know
your right hand is empty, no gun, sun bathers
bathing on the run, and you getting out!

Ah, you should be used to it. You make the thing you
love, and give it ornaments, and tricking out the deck
becomes the rage, and baubles make the being
of the thing! You start again, new private eye
greasing on the move, and all you look for
is bruised light clouded in the mirror's sheen.

5

Big deal you're all alone again with freaky dreams
bumbling through the forest where you find yourself,
the dream fumbling with a club, but don't think
the big freaky Dream becomes the Poem.
The club smashes down the pretty drinks
you and it loved so well.
So you and it and all the sticky failures
move out to that new territory

full of treachery and broken glass,
queer declensions, fields of icicles,
frost, snow, blue gloom and paradise
where you, it, she, he and them balloon
into the verbal network like a rubber sponge
(you and your tangled hair: beautiful!

6

the Poem finds a mutual revulsion
to discuss, and if talk founders on the trunk line
on the rocks of new leucotomy, as some believe,
by the Vilna, by the Don, after black nerve winter
which you know will never end so long as
you and it are arguing with club and claw
you hear the neural network breaking down
transmitters fusing with the voltage overload —

you know it really loves you something dreadful
endogenous depression's not enough
the Doctor breaks in with a message from the Poem
now long vanished: 'Meet me, princess, lover!
all smacked up on the highway
down by the river bridge' the new trap trick

7

The city is beautiful in the evening,
seen from a height, with that traffic
breaking rules along the line of light.
Motorised developments emerge from the Poem that
is the city into the Poem that breaks away from
your dotted white mind, so you are caught in your
emotions like a flock of red lights and the buses
bustling to get through along the pipeline.

You are told to say 'The city *is*
beautiful in the evening,' as though nightfall
grew into a frock of lights to clothe the Poem
that now walks in beauty like the diesel tram.
You, collapsing back to trucks shunting in the yard
of your wide emotion now reduced to metal poverty.

8

You are inside the 'scream'. Yes, it's very like
an empty room with sky-blue holes where the
paintings have been removed for your protection.
No clothing, it's called 'naked' like the 'scream'
in the empty room becoming the house expanding into
a sky-blue hole blowing up to the exact size
of your imagination. Think of television with its
cathode snow above the treeline going blue.

You will search for emaciated verbs to stuff up
the cracks of your imagination for imagination read
horror of the empty room where love is all you beg for
and the Poem has gone to Acapulco for the Fire Season
of the Acapulco Gold and other aphrodisiacs
of its liking, of its best desire,

9

Yet this loneliness only means that the Poem
has gone off to ponder its resources, so let it alone
in the café where it can meander through the lists
of great men and their works. For isn't it you
who feature so brightly in its wildest dreams?
You don't believe it? Yet it's true, for it finds
nothing else to render comfort in that realm
where words tumble into space and get lost

in a cold bigger than a plastic bomb exploding
a silent violet blast in outer space or so
you imagine, yet something remains of 'kindness'
for your fortitude in giving nerve kicks to this poem
who rushes out with other 'friendly writers'
and gets totally lost on the fringe of the blast.

10

Exploring the blast area is like
thousands of tiny microbes having arguments,
so you prepare for the inevitable monster.
To return to the movies is like eating cake, so
easy and so forlorn that tears spring to mind.
Is it cold beneath the Arafura Sea? Will television
pop like smoke bombs across the paddy fields? And then
in our armchair the girls will cuddle us together, so

warm, so drastic, that only our manacles will be able
to prevent us from harm and moral slop.
This is what the Poem will hit us with: is it
good enough to be prepared? Or will lunatics
adopt the mask of eminent professors
and slide us all down into the cloud chamber?

11

So the Poem flutters in the room without a cage,
no message, reach for window, brush the mirror
with its feathered wing. Too much? How much
will the average line pretend, how much tension
will the wire bear before the wire begins to sing,
the tightrope breaks a knot? How much meaning
will your page extend? When the line repeat
defeat! defeat! And whose the feet that

beat against the stair? Climbing to an attic
with a view of ruin and a handy ledge.
When did the wind 'wither through the sedge'
like a madman running fingers through his hair?
Force your hesitance. Make do. Face the
sheet of glass. Despair.

12

Beneath the point of view there's
something like a hole, and if you wait around
it will crawl all over your body. The hole
is called 'prose' and never ends, as the point of view
is named 'verse' and never ceases riddling.
You could do better. Later the girls
will lick you all over like a wet hole.
Sooner than you think the ocean will become huge.

It is better if you leave. Beneath the film
there's a gaping laugh like a traffic accident,
and all your fortunes will come true there.
Wait for the lights to change and jump into the soup.
The Poem is nowhere to be seen, so piss off. Later,
in the bar full of maniacs, you will be given a prize.

13

The shoddiness of the work springs from the obvious
haste with which it was assembled, you say, as
a roebuck might spring from a bush if prodded,
and the vast size which overwhelms the viewer
as an elephant will blot out a footstool,
and then crush it. But more must be said —
apart from the speed which is charming, dizzy,
and at the same time dubious, and the weight

lowering over your shoulder like a cloud of dirty gas,
there are similes, metaphors and gruesome images
all tending to confuse like a martini's ingredients
all slopped together, stirred up and not shaken
in the proper manner, for there is a great
lack of proper manner in the whole shitty mess.

14

And more repulsive than this absence of decorum
which may be just a trick like a talking dog
or a brand new theory of poetics dragged
unwillingly out of a hat and made to squeak,
there is a sour taste and a whetted edge
to the thirsty intellect, as though the Poem
loathed its very medium and thus the world and the
big blue sky which we know is good for breathing.

How can we endorse a monster? Christianity is dead
but something else lives on, and it is our duty
to believe it. How can we adore a dirty head?
We do not masturbate. We respect the 'truth' of 'art'
which is now having its pretty face rubbed in the
shit of politics like a new theory of a talking pig.

15

The concept of the abandoned Poem reluctantly becomes
plausible, and then very interesting.
Like all bad art it is phoney. Goodbye!
At night you could hear the language
burning fiercely, and the heavy traffic
moving about. Goodbye! Oh, how I loved you!
Isn't that what it said? And all this
burnt to a crisp! And where is that Poem

we loved so heedlessly and hoped for so much from?
(Doesn't that whip your tragic sentiment to foam?)
I drank a Pepsi like they do in N.Y.
and that fizzy noise was like how
you could hear the Sonnet feasting on itself.
Goodbye hopeless poems! Kiss me! Kiss me! Goodbye!

THE ALPHABET MURDERS

1

After all we have left behind
this complex of thought begins
a new movement into musical form, much as
logic turns into mathematics and automatics
turn into moonlit driveways — 'form at the edge
of hearing', almost, like a locomotive whistle
late at night becomes a linguaphone and then
jumps into bright focus like a lunatic
suddenly aware that hunger kills vacancy
and means lunch straight away — we mean
poems right away and no fooling.
So I write to you 'from a distant country'

2

Before this complex thought begins attacking
what we have left behind—riddles, packaging—
itself must generate enough good luck for the whole voyage.
After trunks full of shit flung overboard
and the page aflame with noise and verb geometry
I'm ready and lunch jumps into sight and we are off
like a rocket, zooming through the lecture hall where
history becomes a kind of thick paralysis and breaks
down into spasms and morality and all we can remember
through the foggy explosion is how we thrilled
and brought back memories of Captain Marvel
wriggling on a pin, or in the lens' meniscus
held to the niggling eye. (He would have made her
had he shot the shot, or had another try.)
No more literature. The dream is done.
But take precautions: oil the gun, unsheath the pen
and grease the new appointment if you will

for we are not all as easy (as the one who hides
in the shadow of the sun and clicks the shutter)
at the briefest flick of eyelid or the wettest smile.
I have been keeping a stupid vigil in the tower
to show I'm not mad and making notes
as to the behaviour of the lesser sex. Take care,
I'm winding up the broken clock and being jovial
as though the word 'maunder' held a secret in its fist—
but those dreams are laughing
and a new horizon promises revenge.

3

Cool it, with all the friends of scholarship to hand
there should be little fright, so take it easy
riding through the night. So
the craftsman turns away from domesticity
with its pattern of submission, cliché and reproach
and retires to a house in the countryside.
It is English, autumn, smoky and reposed,
badgers wander across the great lawns in the evening
and the peaceful rhythms of another, better life
claim him piece by piece. He sits musing
in front of an open fire, sketchbook at hand,
as the tapestry weaves its message in the shadow chambers
at the rear of that condominium we call his brain.
Is it inspiration? Is it luck? Is it duty,
that sour globe of perspiration on the nerve?
He grows, the nimble fingers fly, the pattern
reels an arabesque across the paper. Five years later,
with a hearty laugh, he is gone from the country;
two years after that we find him dead.
And the tapestry? It is now a joke, a dirty parable
that kids laugh about in school, it is a lesson
that everybody hears and no one understands,
it now hangs in Texas in a renovated castle

and entertains the visitors immensely,
and like some long and boring poem by Matthew Arnold
in which the bloodstained burning battlements of Art
rise up in Hauteur from the sodden Turf
it puffs itself up and explodes all over the onlookers.
It is a bladder bloated with its own conceit, and yet,
rhymed or free, retarded or advanced,
as the poetry of life spirals upward in the smoke
from this great and almost mythical work of art
the skills of horticulture carry on, a million clerks
fill out a questionnaire, the grand pursuit of excellence
convicts itself of nothing, and is praised.
So he becomes the amateur and once again
begins that climb through craft to frightful insight
while all I can do (me! me!) is eat page after
page of this 'plain speaking' in a rhetoric
dazed with ambiguity. You might say that
no career is adequate to my melancholy, as it's
true that no whip is suitable
for my desire, but that's all bullshit
and a different kind of gangster movie makes it clear.

4

Drifting through the gritty, adolescent Western novel
we find an endless buried geography jutting up
just underneath the reader's attention-span
and it seems that voyages of this type have a purpose.
The annual outing of the Literature Society was held
on the foothills near the Epic Volcano, an area
noted for its inhospitable terrain and noxious gas.
Suddenly the mountain-side shudders, belches
and blows up with a lewd cracking noise,
showering the explorers with hard poetry turds
that drive them crazy. These little pieces of lyric
fall like tiny brains from the sky

fertilising the lakes and great rivers.
The heavy unpeopled fields that lie
sodden under the mass of tangled verbiage,
the banks of snow that scud back and forth, these
outward symbols of the mind's recalcitrance
plunge us into thinking again and again
and we drive deep into trouble with our queer friends
in the hope of meeting something vast and possible.
What's it like in there? Do we need confidence?
Is the plague edible? Do the leeches? And we fade away.

5

Ecstasy is the Master of Lunacy and calls the tune
you said, and when he sweated on the bed you told
the essence of the ancient craftsman's memories:
'The boats broke against the breakers, and though
we came to the coast in the season of storms
we had wounded warriors, and the sail torn. At dark-fall
rocks dropped down from the cliff, one breaking
the decking, though without great damage.'
I know this about you, that you do not know yourself,
that you walked half the night across the planet
acting out 'The Last Great Monster With a Broken Heart'
and whole armies were commanded to destroy
and broke themselves against the ideology of peace.
You came home as a wreck of love
and told the voyage of the dream in seven legends
each different from the last, and said 'The Cruel Sea',
and said 'Behind the border, burning beacons,
thus we were worried where to wend on our going.
We wanted green water beyond the reef.
These are the feared: water, fire, rock and foe.'
All that babble gone down the chute of years
and now a tale to stop up little frolic.
A gaggle of story-tellers followed into folly.

How do we sort it out? The gilded lie,
the tempting truth about a pretty boy
who gambled with a mighty tongue and lost his wits?
('as one hog chokes on what another shits . . .')
'The wild men were hidden half out of water
behind the highest rocks of the reef, and with the longboat
low laden, many made the deck. There was much killing,'
tells the chronicle, though without regret.
What would the Norsemen say? being
busy at their butchery, a kind of trade,
and having neither need nor knowledge of remorse.

6

Fate is a variety of religious experience which is
always asking its own questions, for it is only
a reductive problem, or the essential gesture
behind every question that a little boy might
store away for the future when he stands up
in the midst of the great Lesson and testifies
'I doubt that there's a problem left that hasn't
crawled beneath a book, protecting its value
in the manner of a whimpering aristocrat
in the year of the "Red Tide", or can we only bleat
being so deprived of images by greedy Futurists
(of how the Duke of Money sucked a spanner
and called it infinite delight, surpassing beauty . . .)
or whether radical gestures
of the more political kind are fit
too neatly to the hawker's palm and politician's arse
and are thus rubbed between the two as if
the only love we were permitted by the Sonnet
was onanistic and deprived, or is it
hope to crawl out of the hole that language
laid us in?' He is not a child, his face
is rainy by now and the class destroyed, he has

forged a destiny from the language and his teachers
must decide to punish him and lead him on
into those areas of doubt and sickness where he grows
suddenly beyond their narrow estimates and breaks
their shackles and the test record and
breaks into a valiant and vacant freedom.

7

Get lost: it might work in a stable society but don't
try it here sonny; we're on the lookout for mistakes
you'll be the first to go we generate
information in the bowels of the earth
and call it 'Happy Holiday, my Good Consumer!'—
the heart abandoned and the tongue forked,
the language binary and don't complain—
we eat 'journalists' for breakfast and 'authors'
for dessert, and if you're clever you're a digit.
You will be pleased to learn we have philosophy:
'No line of syllables can satisfy the Sonnet's
greed for flesh horizons. One dawn repeats
another morning as though metal mocked, becoming
several typewriters at once, and, uh, the
identity code to generate multiple patterns
of rhyme in the cavities of the computer's fear.
Mmmm . . . music, like a river full of dead
vegetables, and that smell like ice on the vein,
and that paradise of shops. You can make it.'
We came back to that liner
who drew the line at the unreachable horizon.

8

How are we locked into the forme that is
history in the making? Is it a trance, or a way
of looking at life, or a means for escaping
the frilly bits that just go on and on?

At night, when the mothy lamp flickers
and shadows crawl across the lawn, do we
cry and think and dream of a perfect history
and pray that our children will be included
in the small reward that trickles out of action?
Is it too late to stare at ourselves cruelly as we must
if we really want that freedom, or are the little fears
that grow out of human contact and avoidance
and the knowledge of all those terrible old stories
too much even for the willing soul? Is our soul
too late? or weak? or unfit for the prize?
How do our acts and gestures, falling through the years,
shore up the silly things we do, the way we
argue and cause pain and hurt our friends with lies,
and make us grand? Grander than we deserve, we think,
and then sob and break down and no guiding hand . . .
for we have chosen to be free and quite abandoned
and, like a salesman driving to a crucial meeting
in a new convertible, hoping that the number
in his pocket will lead not into labyrinths of choice
but rather to the much-deserved promotion he has
grown accustomed to through books and television
and who imagines dialling and the sweaty phone and
the avalanche that middle age and masturbation brings . . .
like that small and smelly man we lose hope
just at the city limits and give away the game.
For history is a kind of city, dusty in the quarter
where rats and garbage bury our best illusions
so that something old is seen as something broken
and ignored, and any fresh idea or politician's trick
glints over the rim of the new developments
where orphans, children of ourselves and kin
to those we now imagine, play in a cold
and futile light that sweeps in from the sea
reminding us of those even further reaches
where shapeless things toss on a dark wind.

9

I find myself alone in a room full of dirty poems
I find the girl naked under dry leaves I find
I have a searching pain in the neck
I am not happy I am full of elephants
I find the pain congratulating itself
I am going to move to Bermuda where
I believe life is innocent and in the pink
I have some of the questions and a bank account
I know how to kill a rabbit and a lobster differently
I know each lives and dies according to its kind
I have a hand full of fingers they're all yours look out
I think constantly on those who were truly stupid
I don't think we've met I'm sorry was that your
I've had enough of 'literature' God damn
I'm caught in the throes of a merciless poem
I'm having a ball I said look out
I don't have any answers isn't that what they say?
I'd certainly love to is that all right?
I am always about to make a serious study of the word
I, and it's always just too late goodbye mister president
I'm sorry we never met I could have healed your wounds
I think occasionally on those who were truly damp
I hope you like the puzzle that I sent
I think, and after all goodbye Superman goodbye

10

Justice is a kind of rhyme,
though metaphysical and like an epigram.
He who lays his life along the line
will bite the poison pill, and in the throng
the patriot will be anathema.
An afterthought: 'I wish you well.
Goodbye to all pretension. Keep it clean.

Remember Left is Right, and Right is Wrong.
Wipe the gun and polish the machine
and Politics will sing you to your rest.
Keep notes, and nothing more, and make it neat.
The simple honest tone is always best.'
The epigram: 'The shoes will shape the feet.'
Much later, when the season had grown oppressive
with an alien heat, I found myself adrift in the city.
The puzzle glittered in the ruins of the street
beneath a building like a broken tooth.

11

Karl Marx is a comic novelist, almost—
but when we read *Das Kapital* between the jokes we find
there is a theory of religion, then one of philosophy,
a quick adventure and a sordid tale of justice, and soon
a kind of parable emerges like a shadow on a screen:
man is born, grows up and dies. But if this is all he says
we would be cheated, and the authority of the work
is proof of something more than entertainment.
It is like a factory which, on weekdays,
choked and smoking in a parody of industry
yet holds prospect of a new revival of the workers,
and which on the weekend sinks into a profound silence
that embodies not only the concept of the easy
forty-hour week, but also the executive's retreat
from that which, though stained and horrible,
provides him with a pretty secretary, a young boy,
a lunch account, and fears of bloody revolution.
(Don't cry at the end of that novel, it's ridiculous
unless you cry glycerine which is sly and tricky
and all the kids here will love you for it
you witty bastard and envy your 'attack'
or your nerve and pat you on the back and then
leave you to your own devices. It happens.)

And think of this: each Russian movie masterpiece
bears his stamp, more than an individual approach,
which is like—uh—like a buried emblem
of the work itself, a tiny mirror for the plot—
or maybe narrative—and in this frame
the image, drift and meaning of the total work
act out their small and wistful life.
Outside this interlocking blazon, a life-style
called 'the film' takes place happily
night after night millions of times
as wasteful and expensive as a Russian dictionary
and more misleading than the tracks it leaves
entering and leaving your life,
and what is that? Snow, politics, the cruel city,
that goodly pedagogic food you ate—
all right, I'm moving, through a dense topography
keeping an eye on how the colourful natives
act out a plausible way of seeing it
for our benefit as we hike away,
leaving behind everything we possibly can.
Getting out is easy, but how you get in—
say, back through a locked window
into a room and a dead love affair
you abandoned the night your future called—
blue moonlight, vinyl floor, lots of mice,
and three creeps in bed—that's different,
that's destructive like a zoo brings tears easily,
so take it easy and forget the lot: Karl Marx,
the parasites, the lovers and the zoo
and run out into the beautiful 'life'
that awaits you. Goodbye.

12

Love is the most awkward game to play. Love
you, and all the wrappings of repair. Move away.

Hate is something closer to the bone, the crooked shank.
Loving You is what the singers say
crying with a mandolin accompaniment
all the way to the bank. Peace has a symbol
like a dove without a cage, and victim to the hawk.
'The olive branch is easily bent,
and rhyme can very sweetly clothe deceit.'
So he, lighting the drug late at night
in response to biochemical necessity,
constructed a crossword in the shape of an 'Ode
to Genius', in which the legend of a young Poet
screaming in his trendy garret for an ounce of plasma
was finally demolished by the opium smoke
eating into the paint that held his face together . . .
slotted the last clue into the crossword and hit the floor
the clues fizzing like a fuse until the tinder took
the book igniting in a flash of anti-matter (at the moment
that his lover was opening her lovely legs) and a
blast of silver light: KA-BLAMMM!
Love is like a dose of vitamins

13

Maybe you've experienced the feeling of reeling in
a tricky fish? Love is like an angler, or his goals,
obsessively preoccupied with problems of the tide
and plotting out his map against the stars
while fingerlings in countless glittering shoals
play Doctor ('Look at mine!') beneath his keel.
When you're in Love, is that the way you feel?
Love crawls up and knocks you out
and takes you for a ride. So while the poet
casts about for the frightful tribes a cold
current is working against him and a vast and frigid
tide of solid water trawls the river bed, stirring up
muddy images and loose packs of themes with needle teeth,

and far across the Pacific, deep in the clouded waters
a movement coloured with despair is working its way
toward the coastal battlements. A sudden squall slathers
ice across his face and in the shrieking wind it seems
that the dead cargoes of all the oceans in the world
swing up groaning from their silty bed and rise
dripping and glistening with deathly light
into the unbearable metal blue of 'Night on the Waters'
where the sea's face is glazed with platinum
and the poem's promise thunders on the broken coast.

14

Nonetheless I am still too young, or
younger than I was, and it's due to a course
of brain-expanding, or younger than that diary
you can see reflected in my dirty window that explains
everything that's gone wrong with civilisation—
it's a forgettable catalogue of folly and pretension,
it's full of gloom and agonised regret and triviality,
it's like a radio play on television, it's like
electric bath-water spilling out of the beach house,
it's more like Mario Lanza than Frankenstein,
though more like Frankenstein than President Kennedy,
and less like President Nixon than a quick fuck.
I'm like a doodle, or a geriatric's holiday,
and you're like a red bandanna in the spring,
and the war's begun already and it's eight o'clock
and eight o'clock is like a squirt of coffee,
or the end of the Russian novel comes
running out of the bunkhouse screaming
'Get the boys! Get the whiskey boys!'
and the whole town blows up in a blurt of glue!

15

Only ornithologists nowadays write of
blue feathers on a gelid sea
of placid blue, if colours as they theorise
have love of value relatives and ambiguity
and hues are touched with empathy until
they glow with the real uh comparison
of a blue feather on a lake of blue
feathers gelid in the mood of their own unconcern
and 'hating' each other—imagine! hatred tones!—yet
we are stupid because of our binoculars,
our blue spectra and dioptric Ultra Violet
or some other feminine plumage of the 'gelid sea'
so we take a fizzy pill and jump to sleep and
straightaway we become tired in the exhausted
air of our comparisons, and so depart

16

perhaps for harsher climbs. If you could see us
you'd be amazed — riddled with 'the word' whatever
that is, the *oeuvre* of numinous lunch gastronomics
abandoned in mid-choke and throttling on the floor
'like a small and desperate animal'—what can you
make of us, who are so deprived? That we simply guzzle
sound, experience and meaning and are thus disposed
to throw it up? No? That all we mean
is parallels and trizzy metaphysics,
metaphors of loss, we 'quiet ones' who have lost
nothing worse than life assurance premiums?
We who have swallowed 'the best that Western Literature
has to offer', and shat the lot out on the lawn?
Or do *you* propose to give us holidays
in which we can brush up our commitment?

Plump the flabby pillow of our means? Load one chamber,
spin the lock, squeak and tickle the trigger and thus
create a new beginning for the literature
of the cultured market gardener and his gleaming wife?

17

Queer, isn't it, how holidays decline
around the rim of a bowl of ratty soup
just so that you and Caroline can make the jump?
And sorry how the automotive strivings
dribble to a plebbing tack of politics
and tropic mud. But that's the knock, you'll learn to
love it in the end, you and Caroline and Princess
Froth. There's no choice, once the Luger's empty
and no new bullets in the butt. Pick a mandolin
and hope it's rotten, full of secret documents and gas
to thrill you and Princess Caroline Gorilla
Sloppy Makeup Throttlegut and all her tribe.
She dives about with copywriters, pokes her tongue,
and giggles in the pool like a randy teacher
while you and Randy Preacher make the good news
on a rubber bed, inflatable and quite naive.
The hi-fi gear is glowing orange with the blues
and Doctor Threat is rolling up your sleeve
for that final pin-prick into yesterday. So choose:
piggy-back the dealer while he teaches you to grease
up that pole, and hope you reach the Muses at the top
with their raddled whorey make-up and their flapping tits
and hope you get a good and literary fuck
and if you're nice, a fifty-dollar note. Or get the shits,
hike out through the desert with your awful luck
and take your chances with the butcher's slippery chop.
Look at the snappy camera. Say cheese.

18

Reaching the excuse for verbal intemperance we find
the best argument persuades us to strain out from poverty
to excess, though the profit of this striving
is not in the final chapter but in the zooming
between two worlds of action, neither being of interest
without the gasping towards the other, which is the circus
where we get whatever valuables we come across
and it is not 'reality' nor 'art' that keeps us hot
but the idea of 'hurtling', down the road between
the promise and the freaky now. This
argument reaches its senility in poetry
for Yeats is said to have composed his most valuable,
fine, and enduring works in flatulent prose
then waited for the scalpel of his intellect and sense
to prong them with the magic clang of verse and wham
bingo they became lasting works of art that students
still can hardly take for granted like a lemonade.
So we end up with a mass of words far more
enduring than a bar slob and twice as sickly,
and our argument smashes through the window
like a trembling ballet dancer scared of rape
but less afraid of broken glass, as we are more nervous
of the poem that might not wriggle into sight
if we declined the challenge of the technique
of cooking 'prose' first and then stamping out
these frilly 'poems' with all their endearing
and 'necessary ornaments of sense'.

19

So there's a dance, and in its alcoholic daze
the Dervish fights his drunkenness;
there is a song whose chords restrict the throat
as music ought. He enters the Gateau d'Ivresse.
It's his Seven-League Boots, this phrase:
'The gangster and his moll'. They meet,
and pass the parcel, and retreat.
'Love? It's just a passing phase.'
Pleasure fits the pockets of his coat.
Slow guitars collect within his gaze.
Dolls, dull stilted birds, a raw
laugh in a jar, the rusty gun.
When the band breaks up his mawkish whore
collects herself. The cheap dance craze is done.

20 *(after R. D. FitzGerald)*

These are not restrictions, but equipment
for use in experiment or exploration
such as it is well to have in hand
when leaving main roads for open country, though
often thrown away in side tracks that lead into
dead ends. Moreover tradition is not just an impulse
out of the past; it is a progressive movement
overtaking the present and helping carry it
into the future. To step aside from tradition could be
one way of being left soon in some small corner
which the present has already deserted. But poetry itself
always sorts out the poets it requires
and gives the best of them their orders;
so despite the monotony of much that is formless
the very incoherence and craziness of most
that you have to say are not restrictions,
but machinery capable of jacking up the present tense

and marching it along like a heavy sandwich
into the slobbering mouth of the future.
To step aside is one way of avoiding the collision;
to leap into some small corner is another, though here
in the smog of underlying discontent you find
the older Captains shuffling through their orders
as a paraplegic fiddles with his fly,
and this is the activity of mind
out of which poetry and coloured drinks erupt.

21

Undo the past. 'One must be absolutely
modern.' Sure, we can abandon sense
and sensibility, and all the disinterred Romantics
like a wicked boy punching in a stained glass knight,
we can be witty partly because of our vodka slingshots
and that's enough to kick the European jukebox in and
get a laugh. But this 'building' thing, this *Bildungs-*
roman-à-clef, and forests foaming with the puppy love
of seasons . . . this is architecture, friend, and masterful;
we gape to find the cathedral of words so large
that everyone can find in it the works of his favourite
period, and yet you can always strip that work
of ill-framed accretions and their polyphonic noise
without pulling the whole thing down. Is it plausible
that 'strength' lies in age and British feats of arms?
Are these bits the 'real' cathedral? They might have been,
the whole might have been designed by one man and
finished in the one compelling style, but
this is not what smelled so rich.
'The whole has rather grown than been made.'
Here the jungle is tugged this way and that by armies
of depraved monkeys, for we have reached quandary's end,
surely, as such things have a kind of existence that is
almost midway between the works of art and those of nature.

22

Very pat and tricky, and too bad
things are not as easy. For we have been jumping
into and out of prose as an aircraft mechanic
slithers in and out of coveralls: one glimpse of him
enshrined in 'art' has his figure dwindling
down the tarmac to a hazy wreck to prod his engines
into life as a love's labour lost in valves and pistons;
this more valuable snapshot has him in his skin
giving his friendly wife the prod, and is it
any less 'artful'? To get close enough to grapple
with the problem that lies beneath the problem
that there are no new problems you'll have to crawl
behind the frames in filthy rooms where monsters
fear to think about breakfast in case their hearty
breakfast has eaten itself, and that's nothing
compared to what you'll find behind the scenery,
for surfaces are like chrome in that they rust quickly
and must be scraped away and plugged with fiberglass
thus no mechanic leaves a plane simply polished
but he must have his nightmares confirmed
in flame and crash disaster for lack of digging
into the art of the internal combustion engine, though
we are more like the damaged pilot in his new psychosis
and shall always worry the flight plan to shreds.

23

We could point to the poem and say 'that map',
the heart's geography, and words enact
the muscley parable of exploration: on your right
Maugham's club foot which tromps the clay of life into
a lovely chorus line of English prose; on your left
the dead Romantics, gone into that same earth
that took their tears and all their unforgivable

syntactical mistakes. The land is cruel
with existentialists, though lyric poets
wander through like crippled birds . . . but this map
is false and crazy — here the Doppler shifts
convert to analogue then back to pulse-code modulation
information full of news and noise, so the heart's
continent abandons form and drifts out into the night sky
full of parachutes, and we feel the mind's mountains
bonking against our head like knobs,
for the little 'heart' grows 'dark' at night
and lacking infra-red photometry and radar
we rave down along the flare path looking like
an anxious moth, don't we? In the flight plan?
But there you go again, plotted out of your simple wit
and this is the second-level problem: observers
without the keys to fit their own responses
so that a poem is merely rhyme and meaning, or a gift
of gaudy trash, and nothing else. So we slog on
to navigate the fading resonance of our capacities
and find the luminescent map of armies
burning on the plain.

24

X-ray breakfast waits for the man who rises
quickly: it's 4:27 a.m. and I'm thinking about
time: life is a mouthful of barium and it's 4:28 a.m.
outside the streets shake with snow pneumonia
it's 30 below and I'm thinking that perhaps poetry
used to be the shot that flung the faulted bone
across the lens, huh? or maybe that penumbra
waiting for the Treatment at 4:29 a.m.
and so forth. It's hard to find a purpose
for that grey machine they wheel in in a sheet.
The time runs out, for 'oranges', asking
who needs the teacher? who needs the magazine? now that

we have the movies and can sit drooling . . . cobalt milkshake
waits for the thinker who would think his thoughts
deserve the ink they wish to buy. Go on, go out,
be a good guy and buy some 'oranges', get a 'drink'.
I guess I wait around for the Impossible Profile.
Batman! Batman! (the 'Impossible Profile of Desire!')

25

Yet, as the Legendary Profile conforms to a harmony
then falls away from melody to a broken music
you will find a deep attachment to this taste of absence,
against your will you'll be disturbed by the
persistence of the Profile of Desire as it takes on
an enigmatic pertness you could hardly have guessed at
and it will do you no worship to strive against it
for the Profile is more like the tide in its pacifism
and in its bountiful excess as the paradoxical music
develops a lust for the beauty of the ocean and brings
your reachings into disarray for love of its silhouette,
for the Legendary Profile has haunted generations
and brought cities to ruin by its ideology and though
it is very magic and appears to love you deeply
you will find it loves all the cities it has conquered
for a short space of time and showers them
with an air of melancholy that is never dispelled
as its nature is to be more elusive than sympathetic,
and though you may hold it in your hands briefly
it will depart again for its working is mysterious
and has a logic like that of holiness
in its frenzy; thus your deeds will have no peace
and your slumber no tranquillity until the Legendary Profile
is brought by you again into the terrible wasteland
it once inhabited and shall now always inhabit
in your grief, by its absence, by its beauty, by the fact
that its piercing sorrow is forever unattainable
once you have touched its lips and faded off to sleep.

26

Zero is the shape of the volcano's orifice
as seen from above, as it is of the human's as seen
from below, and this witless natural joke is a clue
to the purpose, function and economic value of art.
Something like a nothing is what we find
at the final port of call on this cruise when,
stained and weary, we get a flash like a light bulb
blowing up in our face and right there and then
we know everything about life and the creative process.
First there is an accumulated substratum of fact,
and secondly a kind of thermal pressure built up
over decades of suppressed fantasy. Thirdly,
when the whole thing explodes you have an eruption
and millions of gallons of stuff pour out
into colours of hot orange and vivid green,
material which may be revolting and even deadly
at the time, but which forms a useful ground
for supposition in later ages. And so
while the first burst is primitive and spontaneous
after the style of the Romantic gush of the early
nineteenth century, the later consolidations
take on an air of careful structuring
like a policeman blurting out a list of filthy books
in perfect alphabetical order. And that is all there is—
once the Romantic Emotion has ejaculated we find
a vast bed of cooling lava, bare and empty,
giving meagre nourishment to those who follow,
and baneful and pernicious in its influence. And yet
we are still laughing in the jungle, and this
dream of art is nothing but a loony fantasy.

27

After all, we had left poetry behind before this trip had even begun, and all the while we have been bereft of its silly promises of beauty, as the liner leaves the dock and one sees wavelets, sodden streamers in a million colours, and some damp flowers drifting downward through the clouded water to that harbour mud; it is as though the coast of South America were never to see us again, and as much poetry as we were able to hint at left as a blur on the horizon as a temporary sign, the more beautiful for being the more easily erased, and even this has strength as it is inevitable and what we have been promised and it is one promise that shall come through: that the slate of verse shall be washed clean, that the South American rivers will drift always to the sea, that the flowers in the mud live and breathe for a short time only and then return us to our dreams.

Sonnets from CRYING IN EARLY INFANCY

2

If you think of Bali, that strange
colour stains the horizon. Recognise it,
it belongs to you, even though
it will always be too far away
to be of any use. Think of calculus
and how it has benefited mankind.
You are pleased as well as benefited,
though you're too thick-headed to recognise it.

Be pleased, quickly, and go to Denpasar.
Denpasar is at the heart of Bali
as tiny increments are at the heart of calculus,
though Riemann, Boole and Lobachevsky
long ago ridiculed the role of algebra
in the creation of profitable works of art.

3

It is heavy with the breath of bad images
it is more than you deserve it is easy
like a news lesson in Portuguese it has
a taste for racing alcohol and other
delicacies how lucky you are how lucky
or maybe it reads how disreputable and diseased
it is easy to read like a polka dot it is
madly in love like a silly kid good night

it cries and wastes away utterly
so trendy so paranoid and so infected
you are already sketching its obituary!
so remorseful so immense so damn evasive
while deep in the Mango Trench a team of anarchists
and so on how I love you how political

4

She turns off the radio and listens to the news,
she talks about the 'cultivated appetite' and how
culture is a necessary adjunct to a life
blighted by a greedy proletariat. I guess
her thirst for beauty is a limp disease.
I suppose religion breeds an art that aims
at frigid excellence or graven images,
depending on the climate of opinion that

we can now see from our beautiful balloon.
'Cheat, magician, thief, have explanation
for deceit!' The lady lights her pipe, forgetting
hydrogen, and the soft climate of
South America envelops us in woolly cloud.
Tiny poems flutter from her lips.

5

They burn the radio and listen to the blues. They
saunter through the cultivated gardens like giraffes
and whisper to each other, they are clever,
they build and revel in a culture shock,
they have an easy beauty and a multiple
limp. I suppose they stock religion in a
Frigidaire, and their prayers for the well-being
of the inhabitants of South America are touching.

We should leave them soon, for their dangerous magic
is a cheat, and none can explain its delicate
attraction: they reach a height of ecstasy by breathing
hydrogen and soft playmates endure them. Their minds
are woolly, loud; their speech is full of gaffes. Yet
they are almost lovely because of their beliefs.

6

You love her: she is lovely in her briefs, though
when she plays the blues she does it drivelling
of 'life'. She is touchable in grief, to see her
attempting to turn on the radio is pitiful
and will move you to an elevated sympathy.
She cultivates a walk like an elegant giraffe.
That's about all she cares for, yet her appetite
is not confined. To sex she is polite,

and her strategies are a model of love, for
she imitates the ambush of a thousand softnesses
and will lick your hand like a little puppy.
Beware her cheating, for she gravitates toward
an art that aims at gravid images of profit,
and will bring you down like a limp balloon.

7

The kissy blue chloroform is brief,
an antidote for every failing gesture,
thankfully, and swiftly brings you down.
Then you turn up the radio's subterfuge
and hear the bright flicker as the lady's
wishes grow into something huge and indefinable.
Your most desirable woman leaves for North America,
you find her photo in the *San Francisco News*

lighting a pipe, and guess what's in it,
and it isn't grass. The British Foreign Office
has a file on her attractions in a lilac cover,
and they are always fighting over the exact shade
of meaning. As a playmate she is quite delirious,
high as a kite and nimbus as a cloud. Kiss!

8

Move away, leave the cheating magicians
to imitate culture poorly and to be polite
like Humphrey Bogart in *The Treasure*
of the Sierra Madre, for when they are grave
the blues turn to muzak and the whole party
throws up all over your white sports coat.
Soon enough you find their photographs
listed in a folder code-named 'Caroline'

and no matter how they use their useful influence
there's no explanation. (She will give you
the exact shade of meaning of a sticky
kiss enveloped in a nubile judgment.)
Thank the chloroform: it brought you up, after all,
and all of Europe is now your playground.

9

He abandoned the delusions that culture
strikes you with, avoiding sex polemics, though
the slick and socially mobile ladies are
nubile with subterfuge. They, sweet ones,
have a new altitude, and lick their lips.
When the branch broke he bit the dust.
They have a talent for the game at hand,
yet a deeper lack of age and caution

seems to beg a remedy like 'failure'.
He dropped into the fashionable bar
in mid-flight with a fierce whisper: 'God,
the wife and kids!' and the flock of ladies
are the more beautifully arrayed for his having
said it like judgment, condemnation, punishment.

16

Sex chemistry is elegant and subversive, like
how it comes crawling out of a hole where
the idea of 'Christine' swallows itself
and suddenly begins to bother everyone —
she's heavy, hot off the Paris plane
with her handbag full of perfumed machinery,
with her waterfall of blonde hair blowing
with her embrace for Tony and Louise

especially Louise with whom she has been
intensely in love for centuries
and just like a snap election
the two of them — silly buggers,
they should know better — Chrissy, her machine,
Louise and the hostess kiss and fall in love.

18

Giving up women is worse than animal laxatives,
it leaves you with a spiritual pain in the head
and conforms its shape to a manual of instruction,
a list of spare parts dealerships in New Mexico,
a mournful gift, and how to fall in love with men.
We got up early to look at the river, or the many rivers
reflected in the multiple prism of the strange air.
Men moved like spoons across the drippy landscape.

Golly, said Helena, there goes my sanity! Indeed,
in full view of the dealers assembled on the bank
she stripped off and jumped into the truck.
It was wet when we got back. I think
if we tape the last few lines into the manual
we've got something useful at the end of the river.

28

The cave exists only to be found, and the dark
waits as it has always waited. Chequered aircraft
swing around the pylons in the storm,
my girl leading. She's a good kid. Her eyes
reflect my best pair of empty grey gloves
as a pewter mirror, like the cold
gleaming on the wing. Moisture condenses
in the cave, awaiting tourists or adventurers.

Impetuous planes! The race is over,
three dead, and deep in rainy Cincinnati
the damp newsprint and the metal meet.
My girl passed through the grey parade
with honour, and her Dad clinks her medals
for luck. The Japs move in on the South Pacific.

19

The elements of form go like this —
you bang your head with a brick. Simple?
I am thinking of buying a new Volvo today,
my reasons aren't very clear to me,
and clarity is essential to the form of the essence
where the essence has been transmuted from Katmandu
sealed up in the baggage hold
of a book of Gnostic meditations

locked in the truck of the Volvo
which will not be bought by me
after all, summer is moving in
and Hyacinth has gone off to find a job
i.e. a job like a truckie or a pill
the truckie eats with obvious relish.

26

The automobile is not suited to the rough
track across the dunes, and soon quits.
I ate fiercely at breakfast right there,
on the sand. The flanks of the automobile
shimmer with metallic heat and echo
when you bump them with your head.
I leaned against them while the stormy fish
gathered below the cliffs in a family

of light, as it was early for the season
to expand in bruised cloud and mottled rain
against the rock wall. I leaned against the rock
wall on my descent, and my thoughts were obscure
in that they shall not be told. I was not
suited to the dunes nor to the family.

27

It's quite neat to get away to the trees.
You lose something, but then you gain.
Powerful medicine pumps into the brain.
He avoided the gathered families on the beach
and, skirting a clump of pines, began
his swift descent. Soon he was a speck
on the horizon, and just as quickly he returned,
burnt and gritty, having learnt nothing.

Lately I've been reading books on Java,
and that's another lie which echoes back to me
across the page. 'Beloved, move into the city,
there's lights there for the little people.'
Promptly at dawn I roam about the study, musing,
and laugh at the book of the mythical kingdom.

29

We live in the age of the great nerve statesmen,
and each one has the key to a golden bomb!
Night after night we suffer this
unwillingly, it is like a moving penumbra.
And when you close your eyes and press
the lids with a brick, bright spots appear.
You get up and shake your head, and think
of the statesmen, how their spots appear.

Differently, would be the case,
for they travel frequently and very far.
Jet lag slogs those bastards horribly,
though they don't deserve it.
They're a pack of bathing beauties
lined up, waiting to vomit! They're off!

33

Was I trained to be a nuisance?
The Training Manual is full of homosexuals;
in it you'll find the key concerns
to the great figures of our age.
When they bomb, they are dreadful,
and terror follows them, I think,
like a dog, a carnivore, of equal temper.
Next year, in August, you will fall in love

with a girl who kisses just like Lesbia
who gave a name to an experience
not foreign to the famous or the great.
You, too, live in an empty mansion; in love
you are a child of light, and of hatred,
and you will learn this to your cost.

22

Yeats rises in the breathless air
as simple as a spelling error
and by the time I'm dry I'm furious.
I travel in a sticky raincoat
and when I buy the gallery I fume,
amazed at 'what paint can really do'.
I'm a monster . . . why, your breasts
appear reversible —

If you drink that soda hot you'll foam!
And we see stomach pumping as a parable
like easy for you, difficult
for me. Robert's won the Froth Gift,
but is he happy? Tac tac
goes the pump. He's gushing.

23 *(The Pleasures)*

1. It's easy to be awfully sick, though
difficult to do it well.
2. Plane trips are like eating halva: you get high,
you come down, and suddenly you're terribly broke.
3. Sexual intercourse distends the capillaries
and brings a flush to the back of your knees.
4. I'm thirsty, I guess. Hi. Uh?
Get a drink.

5. It's hard not to hurt the one you love,
though it's easier to kill a vegetable.
6. I love you. I love absolutes. I'm alive,
according to the latest theory.
7. My hand is cold on your neck.
Do you mind? (Move your neck.)

30

Just under the water sheet you can see
dim grass photographs, two prints
coloured to the temperature of glass
that glint from one sky refraction to another.
Between the surfaces a reluctant prediction
for an invisible childhood, damaged by the future.
Under the glass and the broken starlight
the water stained with darkness

soaks into the earth. Somewhere below
a portrait is moved slightly
by a wish or a failure, to form
omens that point into the past
and indicate 'That promise, how
a tiny growth drains all your effort.'

31 (*after* American Graffiti)

Being brave is not enough, this easy
generosity in the loosening grip, in the
strange light which is given off by bottles
when they are tossed from a bobbing boat
and sink, yet do not sink in that
marsh water we have tasted uneasily
and which illuminates our adolescence so that
hot machines are broken and a promise

is a memory as touching as a bad
but well-intentioned movie, though these
artefacts of childhood drifting into age
will never leave us altogether, for our love
even of ourselves feeds on them and on the
endless sorrow of their pressing toward death.

40

If we laugh and photograph ourselves
which is difficult but not impossible
we create a system for analysing humour
and days later we are stuck with it
like Marxism too quickly understood
and thus betrayed. Is a smile a role?
The snapshots make a guess, and unavoidably
a complex answer is building up inside us

conditioned by empiricism. We love and burn
just for a year or so, then take those photos
and lose a precious ability and a sweetheart
and nothing seems the same, ever again.
This dogging loss chews at my heel and soon
years later, we are less than what we knew.

41

My eyes go pale as I grow old, and these
bones, my wrist, are less eloquent than
country radio. I re-live youth asleep
and leave it behind at dawn. In the mirror
there is only me, grey and mumbling.
Who else was in that darkened bus,
driving six hundred miles to a new school?
Only me? I should remember those boys,

but those are photographs, and anxious men
inhabit them; nervous wives cry themselves
to sleep in the country nightfall.
The trawlers are throbbing out of reach,
lost at sea. The mirror clouds over.
The bus speeds through the wet forest.

70

It was greasy all over like a widow,
Dad resumed, and later in the painting
we were ready to remember those sad bits how
Ted was dropped from the team and got the shits —
was that the way it — really? all our youth
we spent and blew up and emulated — so smooth!
is it gone away? who was that sobbing ghost?
pleading? pregnant kids? that fishing trip? when,

like other actions, that keen yet mousy kiss
hits you like a big blue punch it went
completely so that young Ted, if this vista
was really an imitation of his dearest memories,
broke down and cried that he was old, that most of his
friends were dead, that, kiss

71

The Chicago 'Manual of Style' is really neat
when your composure cracks and ghosts
of silly girls come whispering to bother you —
this happens late at night — just kids
out for a bit of fun with a convertible
and a bottle of vodka like in a movie,
and 'Hell,' you think, 'did I do that? Was I
involved with that mad young bitch

the cops were after down at Sunny Point?
Was that me in Dad's truck with the throttle
stuck open, cracking ninety down the beachfront?
With that . . . brunette . . . uh?' Just about then,
on the edge of love and terror, the Chicago
'Manual of Style' appears and takes you home.

50 *(from a BBC synopsis)*

John is handling a tidy affair
with Louise, wife of his friend Robert.
John tries to persuade her to leave
Robert, and to burst with him in some foreign
country. She meets John secretly . . .
she has decided to grow with Bob
but when she laughs at her husband she finds
he has been spying on her. He says.

It seems that he strangles her in a fit
of jealous rage, then phones the doctor?
When the police arrive laughing they find
John leaving the house, and he becomes a murder
suspect . . . but is Marjorie really *dead*? If so, who
really killed — set in London — *killed* her?

51

Hydrocyanic acid was the least of his worries,
as he tried the locked door for the third time.
Christ, Marianne is in there! he thought.
And then the ether closed its ranks against him
and a great flame came out of the pit, calling
'No go! No go!' and it was just as true
as his love for Marianne, which was waning
as the effects of the deadly gas penetrated.

He was neatly dressed, and calm in the face
of crisis, though he had not eaten a thing
since his last attack. Through the plate glass
he could discern his nubile girl friends
flocking to visit him, and many of them nude.
'So this is how it feels,' he thought, 'to be in love.'

34

He was a living legend. He had built
some great structure mainly consisting of art,
though most of those who went through the experience
were knocked around and were inclined to talk about
'a work of skill' and 'admirable diligence',
and thus quite missed the point. Words, paint,
craft, are easily bought, though hard to sell.
Some said he made a million dollars, though

the figure varied, and by the time he got it
he was too far gone to add it up.
Did he really make a work of art?
Did it 'work'? Is it really 'art'?
Is he still alive, or does his 'spirit'
live on in the elegant reviews? Hard to tell.

35

To solve the problem of art and artefact
will you go down to the river
to paint a 'painting'? Will you 'paint'?
Will you paint the girl by the river?
Will you make a painting of the girl?
The light is Grecian, is adequate, et cetera.
He is sitting by the water. No,
he will not paint the girl by the river.

The girl is an artefact, the problem
of the painting is an artefact, is art,
the making of the painting is a problem.
Will you paint a painting of the artefact?
The scenery is well composed, the light
is Greek, is adequate, et cetera.

36

If you're clever you arrive early.
Just before dawn is early enough.
Don't be too eager, heat factories
will be waiting in the foyer.
Outside, through the grimy window
you can see the moonlit Wreck Express
buried in snow dreams, full of vegetables.
You are stronger than a vegetable.

Breathe in. You will live longer than most
members of the vegetable kingdom. Look,
the Ming Dynasty perished. They were not
as strong as vegetables, and you are clever.
You arrive at midnight, full of strength.
Yes; too early, like a fool.

37

The sunlight and the moonlight,
how easy they are! And yet they are more
than carefully structured opposites.
Unlike you and me, they have no
purpose. When we see the sun rise
through the bronze layers of the air
we think: ugh! He did it again!
And when we glimpse that gloomy moon

on the pewter bay flatter the oiled mirror,
or when, on a midnight underwater swim
we catch that ancient glint on the silvered
river of mercury in the tidal silt
dribbling from the heavy metal factories
we smile. We are happy, because of that.

38

It's bad luck with a coughing baby
and it's just as rough inside the pleasure resort
so don't bother with the Mandrax any more.
You'll get to sleep, and find a business there
that you'll just have to get used to once again.
These palaces you build, or auditoriums,
someone forgot to put the windows in and
all night long you're troubled by a noise outside

so that every day at daybreak you find yourself
asking the keeper 'Was that me? Was that
me and my trouble again?' And he answers variously
according to your face, 'It was a flock of birds,
sir, of red plumage,' or he guesses 'That, oh,
that was you again sir, pleading to be let in.'

39

A baby crawling over the rooftops is a movie
called *The Thief of Paris*. On the wet tiles
at night — whoops, he slips, there he goes — another
baby by the sea, he's trying to surf
and the water's rough, the pilot boat
straining at her moorings on the cruel deep
and a heavy swell lashing the rescue helicopter . . .
a breaker, and all his valiant efforts in vain.

Pondering these doomed historical necessities
we wonder at the lack of politics, and think
maybe it's a dialectical process: one baby
we're supposed to love, one to hate . . .
it's called Strain Your Brain, conversely
Put Your Head to Bed.

43

What can history tell us
that the movies can't? Hollywood is history
and we have already forgotten
Josef von Sternberg, even if we saw his movies,
and few of us managed that much.
We all saw *The Invasion of the Body Snatchers*
and quickly went out for a drink. Why,
we've been snatching at bodies ever since,

haven't we? We saw the Indians
dying like flies, but things have changed.
The Indians are making a movie, and it's not
Batman Rides Again. What can the Indians tell us
that the movies can't? How to ride a pony,
how to fly a night fighter well.

45

Nothing new arrives from Rio, again.
The geography prevents it. There is a faded
portrait of a general on the wall,
a short-lived rebellion on the muddy plain
and an Englishwoman who moons at a window
and hopes that something will arrive
but nothing ever does.
A rose bush clutching at the rusty fence

dries into brittle sticks. Far away
across the Atlantic, a storm full of rain
swells like a bruise and floods the sea.
The lady moons gently to see her hopes decline.
Across the misty ridges, behind the breeze,
is South America. Just over there.

47

He's older now, and has learnt the need to survive.
The evening's carefully planned, down to the wine;
his income hangs on a favour. Guests arrive,
important, cautious, not quite ready to dine,
accepting a sherry, behind the uneasy levity
catching a thread of music from another room,
politely not noticing the unobtrusive poverty,
looking to see who sits next to whom.

The conversation drifts: who's been betrayed
by the one you'd least expect; who's up, who's down,
who left for political reasons, and who stayed.
An awkward pause at the door. Not much is said.
The engine coughs, a car door slams. They're gone.
He has a terrible headache. He goes to bed.

44

Today broke like a china plate,
rain and cloud, drifting smoke;
tonight fell like a suiciding athlete
or a bad joke.
I went to bed with a startling headache
and was distinctly no better when I woke,
I remained dumb in the company of those
who were happy only when I spoke.

Something new has moved uncomfortably close,
something not previously seen:
a talent for aiming the poisoned dart,
for detecting the touch of the unclean,
for discovering that, in the pure of heart,
there is something unforgivably obscene.

55

Waiting and waiting, there's an end to it.
Eating bad food, sleeping on the floor,
there's an end to that too. One day
your enemies reach out of your head quickly
and take you to the cold and dirty places,
and you're too old for that sort of thing.
The bad music keeps you there, and makes you cruel,
and you are the loved one you are least kind to.

Waiting and waiting for the good weather,
there's a hard art in that, and a sour man —
too old for that sort of punishment — does it badly.
But one day you wake up and go back home and if you're
tough and lucky you leave most of it behind. Eating
good food, accepting kindness — there's an art in that.

63

In a distant field, small animals prepare
for sleep, under the huge rising moon.
For foreign peasants, dusk is none too soon.
The bombers fade into the melting air.
In a far harbour boats make for their mooring,
in another town the citizens are glad
the lights are going out. The morning's bad,
the waiting news is cruel, the job boring.

A painter pours a cheap and bitter drink
and drinks it down. His hand's unsteady;
on the table brush and pen and ink
lie scattered. Half his work's no good,
the rest is sold for rent. He's ready;
the loaded gun discharges as it should.

52

The war is over at last
and I have been charged with writing.
I have been ordered to write an elegy,
the dream commands, by bruised boys unable
to command a comprehension of murder.
I am charged with a duty, the committee decides,
to glorify the implements of war! No guilt!
But I make a list of all that is left.

The old world is gone, the Coca Cola
and the benzedrine, the rifles eulogised
and stacked at attention. An old caretaker
is oiling the barrels with a rag and smiling.
The ranks of blued steel grin in the dark.
As much as I am able, I promise the rifles are rusting.

54

I know a man who lives in the dark.
He writes in black ink on black paper.
Whatever he writes is wonderful.
He thinks about history. At midnight
in the light from an ultra-violet lamp
he begins to write. The book will be read
by school-children, he decides, and politicians,
and he considers the struggling republics

and the joys of a country childhood. He paints
a picture of raw youth forged into a legend,
a terrible landscape informed with a sombre glory;
but the ground is a turmoil of combat whose name
is murder. Musing on the republic's favour
he writes a manual on the implements of death.

57

My daughter's playing with her bloodstained
doll again. And the wireless is breathing unevenly
in Frank Moorhouse's novel, grieving that the old
petrol stations are unattended, that all the decent
Rotarians are missing in action in Korea,
the only war to feature the Sabre,
the modern exemplar of warfare,
and the ruthless MiG. It's goodbye to the glue

that used to hold everything together,
it's goodbye to the trembling Rotarians
and their bereaved children in the light
of stinking kerosine lanterns, it's goodbye
to the countryside of honourable rifles.
Welcome the doll, the terrible doll.

60

In a crude circle of dust and stubbled grass
children are playing soccer. All else
is olive brown and blue reduced to powder.
Outside the boundary the referee
draws a line, cutting off an easy talent
from originality. A small dog like a movie star
drags a grown man across the field,
and his friends follow, asking what to do

with the stricken afternoon, and why is the man
crying. The circle of burnt grass grows
smaller, and somehow the game is accommodated
in the grip of politics. In a dark brick
building on the other side of the world
a man is carefully inspecting a clip of bullets.

61

The spy bears his bald intent like a manic
rattle through the street. A bitter rain
stains the cobblestones. A clock stops; elsewhere
winter tightens up its creaking grip.
Why does the soldier pace the empty field?
Whose war is this, so grey and easily spent?
Slow cars patrol the autoway, children
stare at you cruelly from behind an iron gate

and a brutish gathering begins, somewhere
on the plains far in the hinterland.
The black clock has been still for a hundred years,
and no peasant bears the luck to win
in this poor lottery. Dull green trucks roll out
and the countryside is well advised to be empty.

62

The exile returns, at the edge of evening.
Branches are bare. Winter has disfigured
the land he loved, and a strange
exhaustion taints the air. He is
tired before his task has begun,
but he pushes on, inland, hopeful.
He, the only one capable of healing
the whole economy, the one with the key

to politics, wanders to and fro, talking
quietly to the people who are reasonably
pleased in the black and diseased cities,
and finally returns to the rocky beach.
The seasons rise up and pass away.
He thinks: there is nothing to be done.

64

A gift to stir up fevered passions,
in a fit to envision a disastrous future
and to tell it as explicitly as possible,
to see through others as clearly as a mirror
but not to see yourself at all,
this is your basic equipment. As for the rest —
compass, map, a traveller's phrase-book —
use them only if you have need.

You have been provided with a wife and child
and a passport, and a respectable position
with a firm of publishers in the city.
As for the stammering, the occasional
failure of nerve . . . just do the best you can.
Oh — pencil, paper, one-way ticket. Have fun.

68

The theme of the magnificent painting
concerns a boy groaning under the weight
of numberless governments, and a troop train
moving off to the front. As the train
moves towards the regrettable border the boy
unveils his grief — a whole sky,
storms, and loads of bleeding cloud —
that is his only story, and he cries.

That is to say the train and the wounded
meet like ships in the night. One soldier
loosens a bandage in the wind as the trains
pass in opposite directions. The canvas
flutters, the dried wound freshens, the boys
wave blindly from the painting of the whole sky.

58

Wine is a suburb, not a manner of speaking,
and in its various forms takes on the attitude
to tissue that we regard as magnanimous.
It is bland and very evil all at once
if this is possible, and bears a resemblance
to speed, whose ties to space and time
it struggles to dissolve. No use
complaining once the liver activates, it is not

the temptingly trivial shade of a dark sea
nor the emblem of dignity; as it grows
in the dark your smile is being prepared,
your hoarse laughter measured and examined;
the body's suburb snores into the late movies
and Central Control waits on the lip of night.

59

Absinthe breaks down into a type of wormwood,
look how it takes on the Excise Law and comes off
second-best, and imagines in a hundred minds
dun palaces for its own decline. It is new
and easily obtainable, though it's been around;
it would like to be more openly discussed,
though a certain dryness of approach presents
problems for the willing listener — your body

has a chemical glow in the dark, and that
blond sheen it much admires. Too much
fear comes into the equation suddenly — it is new,
a fizzed-up whore out for a Sunday promenade
as it is hopeful or blue, but never obvious like
'the milk-green lens through which Symbolism shone.'

72

The lady falls into a slow decline.
Outside the window, fog and winter rain.
A sticky kiss obscures her design
and the junkies drifting into Sydney Harbour
with their splints and bruises are as mournful
as their mothers calling from the mental home.
A drab idiocy clubs these women so that
even the drunks around the typing pool are lurid

and girls that giggle in heat are soon
seen to be the same as those who weep.
The gangsters have a fondness for their addicts,
calling them by pet names and loving their despair.
Negroes litter the beaches of the Caribbean.
The rain is gentle, *il pleut doucement* in your hair.

73

The word 'maudlin' is not French, although
your wish to have it so betrays a truth.
A sickly mist obscures the waterfront
and the liners drifting into New York harbour
from the winter cruises are not as mournful
as the foghorns calling them home.
A vast sadness lays waste to these holidays
so that even 'drinks around the pool' is stupid

and old men brush their silver hair and cry.
The word 'French' is not maudlin, even though
the poets of the period would have it so.
Things litter the beaches of the Caribbean.
Yes, the rain is discreet, painting
these beautiful pictures for your grief to greet.

65

The rich young homosexual has passed
the university examination, and soon expects
promotion to professor. That's 'old-fashioned'
but don't worry — soon the horrible wind,
the brown wind from beyond the border
where vulgarity is a means of pleasure
and the peasants feast on bloody jewels
will rush in and claim the chair!

And whose face will be discountenanced?
Whose addiction to a sexual drink revealed? Whose
dalliance accepted, then denied?
And then the wicked deaths, and then the pale
weather report. In the vast library
the homosexuals are dreaming of love.

66

Look, drunk, you spill your drink
and the slow stain spreads, taking
an awful long time to dissolve your
memories, like being in prison,
being in love, being stoned, and painters
fresh from *La Grande Jatte* or
someplace optimistic; that stain, then
the black washes into purple

then blue, as pale as your childhood
where the chilled weather came at random,
dampened the bony hills and drifted
away. Fill the glass with that sour wine,
take a breath of air from the window
and run for your future like a drunk.

67 *(after a phrase by Laurie Duggan)*

As we sort of step out onto the page the initial
concept of uneasiness promotes the guess
that 'slack humour edges into the factory yard
that good taste abandoned' though
this plausible gesture blurs just at the point
where our humourless imitations push across
the edge of the paper and sort of into the photo
of the ROCK 'N' ROLL CAFE NOTEBOOK specious

images in the mouth like PEPSI, ST. KILDA, 1936
or later, COLO NO. 7 BRICKYARD and too soon
their easy, vacant trends are ready to be borrowed
and swiftly rearranged with the 'glass of water'
which is mindless and thrilling at the same time,
jerking at the snap into clear focus and resolution.

12

The famous Chinese poet finds a home at last
on the Northern Border. The troops, those
still loyal to the Emperor, those few
not frozen or shot, weave the pattern of battle
they have devised with tired economy.
Years ago they rode out into the Northern Border
to find a desert, bleached bones and arrows.
Somewhere someone waits for them, but not for long.

And already the famous Chinese poet
has sent back to Tientsin for green wine
and writing paper, though he presents a bland front.
The soldiers loathe his ideology, but his mind
fixes on a young disciple, and the image of the moon
'glowing like a skull in the waters of the Yellow River.'

74

Once upon a time I had a dream;
I was in a darkened park, alone
with a demented company director
and he was telling me the endless story
of his life (his life hadn't ended yet,
but soon would) — 'When I was ten
I studied meditation with an ancient master
of the Soto Zen school. I wasn't

ready for it. I was too young and anxious.
My head was filled with nightmares, terror
followed me about, and try as I would
I could never "break through". And now I'm rich
and happy, though a little mad.'
With that parable, he left me to my sleep.

75

A faint trace of pumice on the lung
and you're lofty — it's called
the Rat Patrol, a childish voice
pipes through the long corridors
it's not Arizona, no kidding
a delicate cowboy, no glue
and it's time for Christmas bombing
could you do that? Easy payment

on a moth and you're flying
but I'm grounded, that's the clicker!
Bat bat he's happy, no sympathy
bank managers exclaim
and far out west the ruined debtor
runs for his wife again.

78

The shadow of morality drifts over the trenches
imagining itself a biplane in love
a pretty gift looks up at you and blows up
after all, you said you *loved* me, Harold
and then Wittgenstein, Su Shih, those teachers
who left us terribly alone
under the smoky track of the shadow, Harold
that bloody shadow

All too soon it's dawn over the railway carriages
the shadow's deserted, it's about to be shot
there's a champagne party and the firing squad
are all invited; what charming company, you think
and just then you remember something sticky and
unbearable, and burst into tears

79

In the Casino, it's tough in there,
it's dog eat dog and I'm not
invited to the feast. In summer
the eucalyptus trees are smothered with hands,
the tiny bleeding hands insects use
when they want my sympathy.
Cripples disembark from the Sud Express
when it finally arrives at the front.

Naked women poke each other on the beaches
on the sunny Med. Up north it's winter,
and in the muddy trench it's not so good.
I abhor Europe, said the animals,
the animals torn apart by war,
by the stench of European heroism.

80

Come to Lusaka the pace is killing
the surf and grease machine so fabulous —
you call *that* a postcard? That
elfin strain, it's so retractable, and yet
better than an accident that points out
how you will learn to hate Lusaka
as you already hate Mervyn's Elbow
and the bad time imprinted there —

look at that rebellion it's so junior
the way the pantihose ladders as
the army group fails the last exam
and yet manages to remain believable because
they stare at the telephone all night — that's odd,
your eyes go faint and then pop out!

81

How about the blast front? 'No news'
is terrific if your nerve can stand it,
and a group of enemies promises a happy ending
even if the life insurance is a fraud.
But look — a million postures, each political,
and each concealing a sordid glimpse!
'No chance' is like a dirty singlet
and a pig resembles Wittgenstein

in this pronunciation of the Latin tongue.
And yet he was regarded with a horsey leer
by a dozen spotty girls. He was a 'fumbler'
in that blind yet luminous area of metaphysics
where the concept of the real big drink
jumps out of the blast front into your teeth.

84

'The Rhetoric of Fiction' is a marvellous thing
being so close to the title of a movie or a thriller
or a brand-name for a patent medicine — this
'blank' verse could easily degenerate
through a slip of the tongue into a fictive
rhetoric too; and so as you become aware
and snap off the radio quickly the room
plunges into silence and there is only metaphor —

'Seen from my head, the reefer on the reef,
distorted to an image of a hunk of beef . . .'
and you soon realise that you're not alone, you have
the rhetoric of fiction for your adversary; then
there is only the hiss of a cooling valve, as,
inside the radio, a million people are thinking

85

Good night it's the neighbours and the stereo
warming up again — and can you take it?
Remember, you've run out of pethedine
and that strange feeling in your head
is beginning to resemble pain — Jesus, phase shift
through the woodwork at a hundred dB SPL,
and you thought they were geriatrics, huh?
Feel that, kid, and think again.

Is that the stereo? Look out,
it's midnight — once again the light
polarises, and then the knock on the door.
You open up trembling and there it is —
the green light streaming from its eyeballs,
the tears running down its grubby boots like piss.

86

'It's so easy to write for television!
You make a million bucks!' Is that
possible? And what does a guy do when
teased to death by homosexuality in art
and having written a hundred brilliant freaks
he finds the pursuit of excellence accomplished
and a loudmouth fashion getting off the ground
for demolition? Can this kid resist

the Demolition Derby where the Poem breaks down?
And will the little 'triers', those dumbos,
follow him into the technicolor accident
and not be damaged? There ought to be
a parable explaining how it's done, like
writing a hundred plot lines for television.

89

I'd like to throw an epileptic fit
at the Sydney Opera House and call it Rodent.
That's what separates me from the herd.
The hand forgives the cutting edge
for what the hand guides it to do.
The knife has no pleasure in it.
I'm eating my way through my life —
they said it couldn't be done

but here I am in the Palace of Gastronomes
crazy about the flavour!
Moonlight along the blade of a kitchen knife
belongs to the ritzy forties, it's nostalgic
like playing the comb and one-hundred-dollar bill
and calling it the blues.

90

As you get purchase the hate vehicle
you take another quick look at your sister
and the whole cataract falls into place
under the idea of economy at sea
along the edges of the truck
your sister is playing around smoking
with a nudist drinking pot just
having a real bad time in Jamaica

you know you'll make naked friends
in the twilight you're not sniffing glue
between the Principle of Uncertainty
and the invention of Germ Warfare
there you will find your dazed sister
purchase motor conformity.

92

Every frightened smile prepares
blood for the borrowed floor and then
morning on the street disrobe
smiling as she glowered when
you and Dick, do the repairs,
fix the blue, the broken globe
in that storm we know how
to treat, now she licks her smile

it's thunder, Dad, a heady rain
froth beside the drifting dhow
the limpid waters of the Nile
below, beside, a lark, a drain.
Every newt with flickering fin
guesses right, and turns it in.

93

Sweat is a style of the body
trying to tell us something. Listen!
Tic tic how I get envious
of those cool ladies on the TV ads
lolling on the jungle veranda with a drink
and a sticky lipstick while insects
bother the tropic night I sweat a lot
and in a desperate bid to externalise

a talent for journalese I wring out
my neck and get clobbered. Bid! Bid!
And yet the real storm relents,
and hangs about, a style of cloud sweating
against the windscreen of our means, our
deep trivialities.

94

Rod's high on French television. He terrifies
that interviewer with a Yank accent.AAP. PARIS. WED.
POP IDOL ROD STEWART JETS IN FROM L.A.!
After that moony pose, off to Yves St. Laurent,
even the dress designers have names like
famous French poets. Rod's happy, I guess,
under the wing of his lady, and she, blonde,
works it out on a computer in her pocket.

It's all right, Rod. I'm still living in
Gasoline Alley, he says — he falters,
struck by millions of dollars. Goodbye, Rod!
This question has worried sociologists for years:
would we all end up like pop idols, drifting
westward, high over L.A?

95

James Michener thinks of writing a guide book
to Bohemian Balmain, Sydney, Australia.
People are sick to death of the South Pacific.
He quickly flies to Balmain and has a look.
There it is, like a movie! Writers, artists!
The harbour, blue as always, the container wharves
just like it says in the novels, and the lesbians . . .
My God, the *Lesbians*! Bohemia Gone Mad!

This is too much for James, and he flies out.
TOP WRITER JETS OUT OF SYDNEY, AUSTRALIA!
But is that how it really happened? I like to think
of James in the Honolulu Hilton, older and sadder,
nursing a drink by the pool, nursing a broken heart,
dreaming of a pert little lesbian in Balmain.

13

FAMOUS POET JETS HOME TO USA!
How lucky to live in America, where
supermarkets stock up heavily on writers!
Thinking of the famous poets floating home
to that luxurious and splendid place
inhabited by living legends like an old movie
you blush with a sudden flush of Romanticism
and your false teeth chatter and shake loose!

How it spoils the magic! In America no writers
have false teeth, they are too beautiful!
Imagine meeting Duncan in your laundromat —
in America it happens all the time — you say
Hi, Robert! — and your teeth fall out!
And you can't write a poem about that!

RIMBAUD AND THE MODERNIST HERESY

The kind of poetry that I needed, to teach me the use of
my own voice, did not exist in English at all;
it was only to be found in French.
T.S. Eliot

The whole of my admiration goes to the Great Mage,
inconsolable and obstinate seeker after a mystery which
he does not know exists and which he will pursue, for ever
on that account, with the affliction of his lucid despair,
for it would have been *the truth . . .*
Mallarmé

1

Sitting by the river under damp trees
I listen to the wind in the leaves
whispering hatred and loneliness: a spirit
eats into the bones of small animals, I hear
a distant roar like a crowd driven mad,
devouring itself. When it rains in the bush
you get depressed, everything's grey
and the way you live disappears leaving
a blank mind with a slight headache
clouding the edges of the view, and the view's
fucked by your understanding of history, e.g.
this is the century of indecipherable writing,
the age of impossible verse, of wrecked metal,
cancer, bad sex and epidemic syphilis,
cities flaring into cinders, machinery
sunk and rusted in the flowing stream.
So you begin a letter to a certified
criminal — *dear Arthur, this is just a gesture*
like a self-addressed sympathy card.
You should have been at the Poets Ball,
everyone was pissed, it was like
the Left Bank . . . The library is full of

academics, and they're reading *your book!*
How do you like that? When you shout
the sound plunges into the tangled bracken
and the bank of tussocks, your voice
is taken away from you and buried in the hills.

2

Reading books expands the cranial capacity
and with that extra brain you can talk
to the dead, and sometimes in another language
that takes years to decipher, for example
The old poets are drifting
back into the mist: Li Po drowned, Tu Fu
grey and dazed in the bamboo thicket —
they used to hold hands, share a blanket
in the winter, and get drunk together.
That was the T'ang Gang, in the old days,
if you survived the purges you were okay,
but you needed nerves of steel and a healthy
appetite; then battle, famine and ruin . . .
in the eighth moon of Autumn a storm
tore three layers of thatch from Tu Fu's hovel —
'After the disasters of war,' he said,
'I have had little sleep or rest,'
and the rain pouring through the roof.
'Now I dream of an immense mansion,' he tells me,
'thousands of rooms, where all the cold creatures
can take shelter, their faces alight . . .' *You*
should have had such pity on the future,
or were you dreaming of the future, of the
creatures huddling under the river bank,
the rain curtain smoking low on the water?
You are a parable for what has gone wrong,

and through that mirror I see the Chinese poets
bewildered by the twentieth century like children
shocked into recognition of the distant voices,
the rain in the rain-wet boughs, the bright wind.

3

The City, the Book, these ordered lies,
it's part of a grand authoritarian design
to drive us mad, and only the Celebrations
keep us sane: the Fiesta, the Mardi Gras,
Fat Tuesday, Black Friday and the Suicide Follies,
these are our defence against the history headache,
the dialects that glitter in the bookish gloom:
mad butchers gilded out of recognition,
a simpering prince made into a man,
a man made into an idiot, and a woman burnt –
the Romans brew up a subtle broth of poison
and sign their decrees in purple ink,
athletic Greeks compose an army of homosexuals,
Egyptians unsettle the future with a
nightmare weighing a million tonnes
and the Gauls rave and blabber in the forest,
shocked by their destiny: to hack a city
out of a marauding wilderness and see
the suburbs crawling with merchants. Like
Rimbaud, in Aden, buying coffee –
Ten per cent! Ten per cent! Yet that
City's final logic is conceived by wiser men
than those who conquered with the stink of blood
in their nostrils, who spoke a military dialect
that said sophistication was a way of dying cheap
and cursed its own future in a foreign tongue.

4

A mad king plotting horror
in an overgrown field, broken steel
rusting on a hill, a plane tumbling
in the air then bursting into flame,
boys torn in half screaming,
the deliberations of important men
and their reluctant signatures
on a document that soon flickers into ash,
and a war, then another war — these nightmares
are neatly folded in the library,
stacked on the miles of shelves
waiting under the fluorescent glow.
And after that, the poetry selection.
Stop telling me to suffer! Let me do it
my way! The book trolley
trundles up and down . . . Adamson said
he went to Fisher Stacks and saw
two million books — horrible vision!
And that was only Mod. Eng. Lit.!
Sure, I want to be a great poet;
what do I do? Write lyrics for The Mob?
Kill somebody? Arthur, you
would have made a great punk rocker,
says the consolation telegram in French:
'Ma vie est finie: Rimbaud', it's obvious,
and the author catalogue agrees, i.e.
No Translations Held in Stock, see Starkie, Enid,
but we didn't go to Oxford, and we 'have no French'.

5

After the lost generation we find the single
beatnik emerging, it's like Castaways in Space
with a drug supply at the corner store
and we're getting fresh on adrenalin milk-shakes
when the beatnik declines as a focus for the novel
and the word 'hippie' surfaces in the dictionary.
Inside a novel is a growing boy
buried in the print and waiting to get out,
in a diary a man pretending to look
carefully at his youth, on the painting
of the whole sky the fingerprints
of an unwilled and crooked politics.
I look back into myself 'as a visitor
looks at his room and the bowls of flowers
obviously not gathered from the garden
he can see carelessly framed in a window;
the cupboards are lined with yellowed paper
and in a trunk he finds a suit
that fashion forgot, and a broken toy
belonging to a past he never knew.'
I sure could see a lot of gum trees
from our front veranda — 'veranda', that's
not even English, it's Hindi — but not
a single human being, and if I could
they'd be farmers thinking money.
You build your future out of sweat,
pain, deeply-felt experience and alcohol.
I'm thinking of 'falling in love'.

6

Yes, I'd like to believe in a sudden
religious conversion, in the discovery
of inexhaustible energy reserves, a grasp
of sex and politics — all I can remember
is a teacher who taught us some of what he knew,
planting rebellion in a book that snapped
shut, a desperate essay into drunkenness
and a dead poet burning like a virus,
tainting the pages of a thousand magazines —
here is a thin talent shrieking imitation, there
an old man, uneasy with a maudlin respect.
Too near, too far away, not American enough,
confused with an angry complexity,
as simple as a rhyme — here is the art
of counterfeiting in a single phrase,
here is an adolescent growing up crooked;
in the universities, a small profit in a great
decline. In the double journal — art and life —
that symphony begins where
hermetic secrets grow through discord
and resolution to hermitic silence.
Art in the bookshop, life in the bar
with the dancing girls, or vice versa,
when the audience piles up everything goes
quiet, waiting for poetry to happen.

7

Three times in one year I searched
Batavia (Jakarta) listening for the ghost
along the dull canal. Machine-guns
clattered in the avenues as he had planned.
Baudelaire, dwelling in his 'too-artistic milieu'

could pander to the story of a voyage,
and lack the grit for further wandering;
Mallarmé could edit fashionable magazines
and imagine a Platonic Minotaur
behind the empty mirror, the moral being
that the Book, like great music,
falls short of our desire. *You*
talk about a theft of fire, you that are
consumed, and driven into dark. I drift through
tropic endeavours where deceit and betrayal
of temporal power is to be excused in favour
of a greater politics. Reading books.
I look for something generous,
beautiful, and profound. Rebel, Revolt,
Revolution — in these contradictions
there is a germ of peace, but at the cost
of war, and in that broil of horror
the possible gestures of love are shrivelled up.

8

Crossing the border of exile
you break off from the common spirit
in the certainty of torture. Where
is the reason in that? It is a lesson
where suffering may be seen to extend
into the rule of law, and blight others,
or tear out the roots of a milder rhetoric.
He shared with Baudelaire the circular belief
that there is no salvation without sin
and that no deed has strength without adversity;
so no vision weilds a cutting edge
without the stone. Proof? History, where
the flowers of M. de Banville wither
on the slopes of a laughable Parnassus,

or where the poison reaches out
to find its level and the theme a full
throat of harmonics in another field of poetry,
or proof in failure and destruction,
where the new metal
finds a dozen alloys in the flame.

9

The same sun blasts the burnt
volcanic cone of Aden, in a time when
British helicopters decorate the sky.
The tourist boat pulls up, and there you are!
A strong line can bring down a horizon
in flame, though no fabulous creature
stirs the ash in the cooling crucible.
Where your footprints lead me through
arenas of history, guns prop up the state.
I have business with a more subtle
oppression, not with this mechanical brand
of torture. I track the scholar through
the hagiographies and find him seeking
money, mathematics, engineering with
commendable excess and a lash of private agony
to keep the bookworms at a distance — the short
length of history, envy, imitation paddling
the shallows of a 'great talent' — and fugitive
from those ghost images which shoaled the sky
at Harar, and which begged remembrance from
one well loved who moved
too far away, and always under the shadow
of a morbid and inexplicable shame.

10

‘A meteor that blazed across the sky
of poetry.’ A falling star, fallen angel,
child in love with drunkenness.
A shadow. A scholar, a teacher,
a mask for violent metaphysics.
A slave beats his master. Like an
allegory badly out of true,
an old song continues under the lamplight.
Somewhere far away a weary man finds
nothing under that sun which brands him.
He learns a pointless trade, and finds
a worthless bargain in the desert.
Back to the café, and the drinks.
After the coffee, you realise
it’s not suicide, it’s just
‘giving up’. That’s not a meteor —
that’s an engineer! It’s terribly simple.

11

Departure into new affection:
Find yourself another boy-friend!
A towering cultural edifice: twenty poets
in a heap. And they were all —
just a minute ago — polishing their
metrical instruments, based on a device
that folds up into your waistcoat pocket
and, when extended, measures alexandrines
quickly, to an accuracy of a single syllable!
The child father to the man finds
suicide. The scout rambles far ahead
of the platoon . . . cut the line, forge on,
treaties of surrender pushed through,

then the bargains go rotten
and the natives rise, foaming . . . honour,
a very colonial concept. The profit motive
is modern, direct, and very attractive.
The lonely sniper broadcasts
information in a foreign tongue, and
the rabble bring a tardy homage
to the grave. *A rich young painter*
posed naked, hiding his face behind
a photograph of your face, while
half a world away a rich woman
laughed at the joke. You have
seen these people before, eating you up,
it is like a nightmare.

12

Some have built a theory on the ashes
lacking native resolution, and now a paste of
bullshit obscures the surface of the legend
that cast out flattery and took rhetoric
and wrung its neck. *To follow you we must*
desert, or suffer Santayana's condemnation
of those who fail to profit from the
lessons of history. I'd like to talk about
that ghost waiting in the garden
in the rain. A dozen critics are thrusting
different tickets at him, the young President
of the Media Poetry Action Group is asking
the ghost to come to the party, a ruck of editors
need his endorsement, and will forge it
if he declines. And the rain dissolves
the group photo of the Chinese Poetry Team —
Li Po back left, the one with the Rolex —
into a grey sludge; the ghost
scribbles a quick autograph, and fades away.

13

Let's invent cubism! Let's invent
dynamite! They did. Modernism
floats out onto the quiet flood.
A new century begins. Machinery
lays waste to the winter landscape,
but the poets are all in the brothels
mixing technicolor drinks and winning prizes.
Out of that testing flame . . . it's as though
a fine legend were scorched in a radiation storm
and Superman awakes — not the Prince,
but the Slime Machine, the Monster
from the Black Lagoon. And then
the legions of the walking dead
move out in mutilated sleep
across the face of Europe. No book
has ever changed the destiny of stupid men.

14

It's like this: 'Having a good time
is not as easy as you think, when you're
living out a living death.'
At your distance from the human
no one's having fun. At the beach
young men bake their skin, the tide pulls out . . .
a child wears horror and humiliation,
a jewelled manacle, for twenty years of exile
into pointless death. *Why did you do it?*
Brutal, extravagant, pretty,
face like a peasant — no, an angel,
hands like a peasant — *what a*
nasty shit you must have been. Sodomy! Lice!
I have crossed a different desert
under the same sky, the landscape
waiting like an empty glove. *Arthur!*
Give it up! Come back! Six a.m.,

should I go to Bondi for a swim?
Fresh air rushes across your face, but
literature buzzes in the back room
like a warning from a Casualty Monitor.
The Nurse jumps up and spills her coffee,
another patient dies for whom no one
writes a poem. Another
day begins, and the traffic.

15

One hundred and eight years
since he told de Banville to adopt
the telephone pole as his iron-voiced lyre —
you thought yours was the Century of Hell!
You hadn't lived! Fifty bloody wars
have stained our sleep, and poetry
has sickened in the face of economics.
I've loved and hated you
for twenty long years. I've had enough.
I've drunk enough of your beautiful deceit.
'I have lived between the covers of a book.'
I've never been a philosopher — except
briefly, at seventeen, when I broke down
and made a choice: saint, lunatic or poet,
but not a front-row forward — and picked myself up
and went on with the business of excitement.
Arthur! We needed you in '68! — you
cannot accept this burden of pity.
Learning, where the deeply human
is the object of a fierce knowledge,
can reach an imitation of the style of love,
but in that future under whose arrogant
banner we have laboured for our own rewards
we shall both be gone into that
unforgiving darkness.

ODE TO COL JOYE

You open your eyes and realise
it's the morning of a summer's day in Sydney
and it's going to be — not a John Betjeman day,
though you can hear church bells
    faintly across Annandale,
and not a John Forbes day, though
the first thing you notice is your suntan lotion
on the dressing table beside a beach towel
decorated with a crude scene of coconut palms
    and a jet bomber
pencilling a faint vapour trail
    across the Malayan sky
                                        no,
not one of those days, and you think about
    the exact shape of your headache
and the taste of the first disprin of the day
and you wonder if it will be fine or cloudy
    and then
the hollow yet insistent sound of a Coke can
    rolling along the gutter
fills you in —
            it's a *Ken Bolton* day!
                                            and,
as if to underline the accuracy of the hesitance
of your mental sketch of an approach
    to the definition of the day itself
a paperboy shouts something like
                                                New York!
    New York!
(you're not sure . . . perhaps 'No Work?')
    and when you get up
wearing your shortie pyjamas
    you find a note on the kitchen table
        on a sheet of blue and white paper

to say that Bill and Kerry have gone to the beach,
        and after that
a lunch party at Anna's, hard-edge
        coloured cocktails!
to which *no one* will be invited! you
                                                                        gasp
as the water gushes
                                            cold out of the shower —
it's enough
                        to be having a shower
                                                                    in the hot
blue summer morning in Sydney, an ambience
that no Melbourne poet will ever appreciate,
        and you almost
blame them for that! but 'blame' is very
        un-Sydney, so you
smile and finish your shower
having adjusted the warmth of the water
        thinking of Bondi Beach
and of the poets you know who will not be
        planning to go to Bondi today, after all,
                they never do, but
at least one of them will be planning to
        write a poem
about not going to Bondi!
                                                        and it's perfect!
as perfect as a milk-shake at the Bondi Pavilion
whipped at exactly the right degree of chill
        to get a froth up — a skill
that no Brisbane poet will ever
        comprehend —
                                    whoops!
                                                            you slip in the shower
but regain your balance, and that too
        is a metaphor!

that no Canberra poet will ever endorse,
                                                            and
in a leisurely and very Sydney way you write
with a soapy finger on the wall
      of the shower recess
an alternative version of Laurie Duggan's
      'South Coast Haiku'
            a 'North Coast Haiku':

The milk can
falls off the back of the ute
crushing the Bonsai Marijuana

      but you condemn it immediately
for being too
      political
            and the shower does the rest —
                                                            no,
it's not a Les Murray day, though yesterday
Doug Anthony's name was all over the news-stands
and you found a mysterious copy of *The Land*
on your porch, bleached by sun and rain;
      and it's not a Bob Adamson day,
            though last week a bank robber
ran amok and was shot to death just
five blocks away, under a windy Sydney sky
full of light and utterly lacking in remorse,
      as Melbourne skies are never
            lacking in remorse
and it's not a Poets' Union day, though
last Sunday was full of bickering relatives and
      nothing much got done,
I guess that was a Poets' Union day,
      though it lacked a 'chair'
we have a 'chair' today and I'm
      sitting on it
                  it's not

a Sandra Forbes day, though the light is so
pretty as to be truly beautiful in a very 'Sydney'
        and 'cool' manner,
and yesterday I read a poem by Auden ending
        'I love America,
so friendly, and so rich!' and I thought
it must be a John Ashbery day, though 'John'
is hardly 'friendly', though perhaps
                                                            'rich'
and rather too 'American'
                                            it's the kind of day
where I notice that my Renault —
        a beat-up Renault; how
                Sydney, and how French! —
has the name RENAULT on its side in chrome letters —
how metonymic
        that the name of the object is seen as
being part of the object to which it refers
it's a day for writing
        a self-referential line like this
and getting it done in time for a coffee
        and a Chesterfield filter cigarette
and watching the smoke-ring blur
        in front of the window
                like a circular argument
                        about Mannerist art
as confused as the smoke now
        dispersing from the window
revealing a view of —
                                        yes, it's *Sydney!* and a
small figure in the lower left-hand corner
crudely sketched with a Faber 4-B pencil
        and labelled KEN BOLTON
is gazing through a window at the viewer —
        yes, *you!*

and from his sternly-thinking head issues a balloon
with the words
it's a
John Tranter day
not like last Monday, for example,
which was serious and very
Alan Gould, or maybe Kevin Hart:
a stranger in the bus said severely
'I ran into Wilson the other day
in the Common Room,
and I gave him a piece of my mind!'
(in my pocket there's a postcard from Martin Duwell,
a volcano rising from the sea near Rekyavik) 'I'm
an Anglican,' the stranger says
and you notice the way the light gleams wetly
from his glasses
'but I'm not your average gutless (. . .)'
(obscured by traffic noise)
'No!' he says loudly, 'I'm
committed!'
and his friend looks at him as though he were mad —
the Anglican, not the friend, though
he looks a bit funny, too — maybe
it was really a Don Chipp day after all,
wherein morals, politics and literature
commingle
like the ingredients of the hard-edge cocktail
that Ken is now drinking with an obviously
'non-committal air', thinking
'Maybe it's a failed Rodney Hall day,
that the earnestness of the air
is inadequate to sustain . . .'
but it's not,
it's a day for writing something 'fresh'
for *Surfers Paradise*
and that makes it a Col Joye day; that,
and the bright air
glistening with poetry and the desire to please.

THE WINE BAR WOMEN

Driving in the country clears the mind, and soon
you're thinking — what should you buy for a woman
who's deeply involved with a young girl — a doll? A
bottle? By now they should be badly drunk and
making an exhibition of themselves at the wine bar but
you've left that scene behind at the Mental Date Line.
As a jockey's error brings grief to the races, these
women adorn the wine bar with their fervid passion
like a froth of cut flowers in a jug of ice. One
slides drunk off her chair — turning quickly,
the waitress drops a carafe of moselle and it shatters.
Driving fast in the country is like hopeless love:
there are no stop lights out here, and when an accident
threatens you have to trust your reflexes — braking fast
you see the darkness at the edge of the landscape
spread across the sky like — *you're skidding badly* —
like a stain of satay gravy down a new poplin shirt,
reminding you that these women hardly exist outside
the borders of their mutual lust — you come to a
shuddering halt in a cloud of dust and a silence
gathers around you: they're both pretty, and desirable,
yes; but how is that significant? Doll, bottle, that
foaming aphrodisiac: it's hard not to hurt the one
you love — what am I *saying?* Confused, you gaze up
at the glittering constellations and realise that a
fine white powder is settling on your hair and clogging
the air filter of the two-litre engine — the ignition
coughs and with a harsh bark from the exhaust
you're moving swiftly in the direction of both women
with a thousand miles of dusty road to go.

AMERICAN WOMEN

A wheel cranks in the forest, brilliant cloud
unrolls above the tundra, and in the silence
a man thinking of a rifle-bolt sits upright.
A woman drives a big car right across town
to the supermarket, fish hack and nibble
at a bloated body at the bottom of the river,
the police workers are shooting the steel workers
the cities boiling in layers of radioactive gas:
I'm drinking whisky and watching the third re-run
of *The Quiet American* and *Tom Paine's Revenge*
and *The Spirit of the American Revolution Gazes,*
Horror-Struck, into the Mists of Future Time they're
treating broken veterans for a new brand of syphilis
impossible to cure and a terminal addiction
while murderers shudder to the new music
'I ain't gonna lay in Maggie's bed no more'
butchers on holiday hunting in the forest
masturbating and reading *The True Confessions*
of a Truck-Driver's Moll while their teenage
daughters are writing phony postcards
from the Coast: suntan foam and fancy fucking
in the surf we hope this finds you well
and wish you were here et cetera love signed
The Gang and you go sick and dizzy and in a flash
you see how your children grow up at a frightful
speed and live out their lives with difficulty
and become old quickly and then die one by one
and then the thing begins all over again from
the grinding of a wheel in the silent forest
from the beginning of the first reel.

THE UN-AMERICAN WOMEN

One, they're spooking, two, they're opening letters,
three, there's a body at the bottom of the pool
labelled 'Comrade X', and you've been asked to
speak up truthfully or not at all. It's like Einstein
lolling on the lawn — somebody *gave* him the telescope,
he wouldn't 'buy' one — and our investigator has him
trapped in the viewfinder. Albert! Tell us everything!
We won't blame you for the Atom Bomb! After all,
you're dead! Four, cancel the code and burn the cipher.
It's no laughing matter when the shit hits the fan —
why are you grinning like that? Are you now
or have you ever been a woman? That's a tricky one,
I know you'd like a stiff rum and coke and ten minutes
alone on the the patio to think it over, but
the G-Men in the back room are getting anxious;
the Mickey Finn's invented, the hand that
feeds you's quicker than the eye, and in a wink
the powder's in the drink! Our Leader's dozing
in a tank and in his memory we labour mightily.
Are you a German Jew? We sympathise; do you?
The Memory Bank is sad tonight, it's asking
for your friends, they have a future there.
Let's share a Pentothal and take a ride;
the garden's full of Government Employees
but I'll hold your hand. You make a movie,
I'll write the dialogue: One, we're laughing,
two, we're breaking rules — I'm finished, you're
dead, and as the cipher smoulders on the lawn
a cold glow rises from the bottom of the tank:
our Leader starts to speak, and so will you.

NINETEEN FIFTY-EIGHT WOMEN

This low-profile journalism based on a freeway —
my thoughts continually in front of a woman's
belly get dazzled and tired too soon — she's
not doing anything to help me wake up except
tickling — Toad Autumn, then the summer of the
washing machine full of bad food like a brain
turning in a widening but pointless circle
on a diamond bearing: 'Hi, Jim! Christ,
you look just like a farmer! *Unhhh . . .*'
A foul boiling noise from the shadows, then
I got thrown off the bus for assaulting
a woman. 'When the war was on, *boy*,
we really had something to do with women
that was useful, if seldom appreciated.
We were all stone drunk, on sherry, mainly,
we used to get in the car and just go out
driving, for about ten or twelve hours,
and see where we ended up. Right? In the dark,
near a swamp, with old people standing around
curiously. Then we'd drive back?' If we could
find the way, in the dark. No maps was a good
rule, but it led to spontaneous ejaculation
and headaches instead of a close talk.
'We'd take any old freeway, and just go. Right?'
The woman's belly . . . no, she doesn't sweat; at least,
if she does, she washes it off again right away.
That makes me feel better. Then one headache powder,
mixed in a real big drink. That should fix him.
He's fixing the machine, with the 'Silent
Bearing.' The diamonds glittering, and the night.

THE REVOLUTIONARIES

Look in the mirror: everybody's gone,
the black limousine dwindles down the drive
and vanishes, leaving a twinkle in the bushes,
or was that a gun? Do you think we were
invented for a future that failed to happen?
The make-up fits us like a second skin.
Open the tequila, let's drink up and get dizzy!
We've just arrived and unpacked, and you're
smoking reefers, you were always too eager . . .
now you're measuring the drowning pool!
Let's use that ice-pick for a paperweight,
and bring him coffee on a tray . . . a white
stucco wall, cactus, a venetian blind,
a zebra coat of sunlight on the bed, and you
dolled up in orange lipstick and a new print dress!
But why are we here again? And why is the camera
staring at us with malignant eye? The hot lights
go suddenly blind and the blood-stains disappear —
we're back in the 1940s and the surly Mexicans
are crowding at the door, it's all over!
Why am I laughing? I'm watching my obituary
develop like a stain across an army map —
now they're cheering, now they stop, shocked,
as somewhere in the crowd a news photographer
loads his magazine; and then the numbers
flutter from the calendar . . . one last
dip in the pool, darling, and a quick drink —
tonight's the Premiere, and when our future
flickers into life we'll take a deep breath
and walk out into the sunlight, free at last.

BUTTERFLY

When she was fourteen, she says,
she ran away from home, at sixteen
she bought a big bike and hit the road,
moving from town to town, looking for
something she can't explain.
Later, with her fluffy blonde hair
tucked under a cap, she worked at
fixing computers for a living.
It's just one weird thing after another;
an odd life, she says, for a farmer's daughter.
Now, briefly, she's alighted
behind the counter of the aquarium shop
to wait out the winter. We sit and talk
while the fish gape and kiss the glass
in a bother of colourless bubbles.
Her blue eyes are wide awake and dreaming:
she's inside a huge television set
under the sea, surrounded by a movie
of a coral reef where a million
coloured fish flicker like confetti.
She shows me the book she's reading:
see, she says, when a butterfly
breaks out of the cocoon, it is already
delicate and pretty.
She lights another cigarette, stares out
through the rainy window at the street
full of showers and the heavy traffic
stalled on the hill,
thinking of the open road,
sunshine, and the next flower.

LEAVIS AT THE LONDON

You need the money — your way of thinking's
going out of fashion, and you're growing old.
You need the make-up, and you need
the wake-up pills before the bombing run;
the flak is active tonight, you need
a glass of something sparkling and a deep
breath before you're ready for the fray.
On your way to the affair in the back seat
of a taxi you catch a face in the mirror —
bandages and a black eye, is that really
you? It's not Humphrey Bogart — you
should have gone to Acapulco like
mother said, but no, you had to take
the youth cure, then the bandage
loops across the screen spelling out
'Mad Dog' and you guess it's true.
The shark pool looks inviting
when they turn out the lights,
but that's for after breakfast —
breakfast on the terrace with the Krazy Kats,
after the test of strength. Say goodbye
to the Kodachrome mirage and the heavy
petting, from now on your career
shrinks to a point and your many enemies
gather like a gerontology convention and
whisper. After the Monkey Business, after
a famous middle age there's nothing left
but the engines turning over, the crew waiting
in the moonlight — and when you take off
the shadow on the speeding tarmac drops away.

SARTRE AT SURFERS PARADISE

I've been lonely for years, writing in the attic
and I owe myself a treat, so I get anxious —
really anxious — and then collapse — I mean
relax — and *you're there*! No, it's an optical
illusion, I'm cruising for a bruising down the
Rue Mort — you don't know me yet, me with my
gift wrapping hiding a heart of gold — holy
shit! — there's a beatnik party, it's the
'Speed Readers' rehearsing for their graduation —
look — they're turning into Acid Radicals . . . no,
nobody's reading, and they all look healthy
despite the exceptions and the junkies and
the speech that threatens: we're us, you're
you, it's *that* kind of party, and
I get a hot flush when the cutest kid
on the team screams 'I'm Teacher's Pet!
I'm Okay!' and the students argue:
Is Rum and Coca Cola a new duet,
or a dialectic? or a way of dropping
cheaply through the floor of the visible
world? 'I wrote a letter to my friend and
on the way I dropped it . . . who picked me up?'
Not the strobe, not the psychotherapist, not
the existentialists cuddling in a corner,
not the girls flashing like a double negative
that argues till the group takes off . . . it's
'Karl Marx and the Moonies' and I'm anxious —
you're not there among the optical illusions
and the female impersonators — anxious
but happy, dancing in the dark.

FOUCAULT AT FOREST LODGE

Your good taste is so packed with reading
you can hear a coin drop at fifty paces, but
is that how infatuation heats up to the pitch
of lust? With a trick flame and a gas tank?
General Paresis and a pack of cronies
are practising the Blitzkrieg Variation —
'A frontal attack on the Lotus Eaters
and you're home and hosed.' Our guide
to the good life is a drunken junkie, half
girl, half executioner, breathing gas, who
fucks like a disco wizard and exemplifies
sheer speed as a final virtue, eating out
with a rush: that's how tonight develops
into a drug catalogue blazing in the
waiting room where I get a crush on
Suzanne Pleshette and in that flash
rise like a broken bottle into the light.
The mob of men, dazed in the Ladies Lounge,
inhale a bright idea: *We're* not slack, we're
paralytic! For twenty cents and a wet kiss
you can take a gun and kill an alien invader,
for a dollar you can overhear a fat man
mortified, but this is only the rehearsal: by
midnight the loonies have arrived, hand in hand,
it's the real thing raving with a purple head
and a lesbian affection for noise. The jukebox
plays 'My Foolish Heart' over and over, then
breaks, and I get emotional again — we're
smoking in the hotel carnage while our future,
thinking deeply, waits for the music to begin.

ROLAND BARTHES AT THE POETS BALL

You are painfully conscious of your discourse
reified into sudden vomit and the applause
fading down the coast past Wollongong
where D.H. Lawrence danced the mambo
with a naked miner's wife — these ambiguities
cross that fine inscripted line
between the band-leader's tuxedo smile
and the waves of sentimental music — 'behind us
towers a vast edifice' — now he's feeling fine
and the Chocolate Wheel routine begins:
one ticket, then another, and the room
collapses into damage like a Mothers' Club
howling their metaphysics in the yard.
He's fumbling for his notes, the amyl nitrite
flashing behind his eyes from right to left
then the movie ploughs off the tracks and you
crawl out of the wreckage with a multiple
fracture — your metaphors flailing at the glare —
and the audience diminishes, one by one,
drinking more as they disappear into history,
the gay bars on the edge of the city raving
goodbye. You know you're losing more than
an expense of rhetoric, your life is magnified
behind a dropping bottle as your vision tilts:
ashtray, glasses, a wet packet of cigarettes
slide off the table in slow motion and
politics are acutely personal to you now
as your brutal hangover graduates in the arms
of an older woman mumbling in her sleep:
'I'm the Guest of Honour, and I'm going home.'

ENZENSBERGER AT 'EXILES'

At the back of the bookshop a Karate expert
keeps a pot of coffee brewing, in the window
a man exhibits his bandages and the lights
flash red, amber, blue; all night long
the sex magazine quiz gets filled in.
What am I doing here? That cloud layer
threatens nothing, and speaks casually
of a distant beach; everybody's laughing . . .
they trained beautiful men and women
to meet me at the airport, they
follow me around and buy me lunch,
they point out the misfits and the deviants
and keep me amused at parties where young men
fight and make up like emotional Brownshirts.
In Martin's Bar the topless waitresses
are all sober, their perfectly matched tits
jump at the drunks while upstairs
a poet listens to the race results,
next door at The Balkan a cloud of burnt fat
gushes up the ventilator; these
are the good times, Australian style,
this has become a new vernacular
and waits for my Adler to turn it into German.
Europe is a ruined Paradise buried under
books; here, nothing important was promised.
I'm drinking coffee and writing
in English on a piece of crumpled paper;
soon I'll learn the native dialect and ask
Where are the ovens? Is it true that you never
learned to kill each other? Are you happy?

APOLITICAL POEM

For you out there in the agricultural
colleges and on the membership committees of our
best because least endearing literary salons
the future gleams bright as the dentures behind
a Californian smile — like a skinny-dipper
jumping from a tub of ice your cares breathe in
then flat as a bag of crushed loot
reappear from beneath the wheels of culture
explaining everything except the perfect
concept of yourselves as the ruin of a rope
factory or a Big Mac chucked under a truck.
The shape of literature is crystal clear today
and assaulting a Mouseketeer is less rewarding
than a drink with Gerry Wilkes — a living death
waits in the jungle or it's a silent pool
player's trick with spittle and after that
encounter you're no wiser than a grant
application in a foreign tongue, an idea of
luxury more dazzling than a South Coast beach
bum's hangover though on the trek the idea
of slum demolition entails you'll find a way
of cancelling the smoker's habit of legerdemain —
in short athletics are too brief and epistemology
too Hellenic for the buzz we'd be happy to acquire:
hanging from the picture rail supported by
codeine phosphate and its many analogues.
What the liver knows the mind entertains:
underneath the sparkle on the surface
it's a lucky habit or a Chinese epigram
entitled 'Erskineville, 1959'.

TELEPHONE

You know it's dumb hippie magic, but you try
the Zen Bingo Method of Prediction
developed by a gambling vet for the Womens Weekly.
Your girl-friend goes catatonic
and leaves home, so you burst into tears
like a pop star. 'You will grow old, then die.'
So what? The morning after you have trouble
focussing, it's a vertigo attack but you're soon
rehearsing a complex language of invective
that you must have learned in your sleep,
a dialect so eloquent it fills your day
with its brilliant and torrential speech
then you put your clothes on back to front —
it's in 'My Book of Silly Things to Do' —
and the Pop Rocks go off in your mouth,
that's the Chinese Breakfast coming into fashion
and you're feeling great; at least
better than yesterday — remember that?
Those terrible things you said, and the way
they looked at your fit of temper then
looked away — remember? Good, now
things fall into their special place:
that blonde falling down the stairs
of the restaurant, the famous book
falling open at the page where your name
appears as the main suspect, and the handset
dangling from its cord saying 'dial-tone',
'dial-tone' until you could scream.
Somewhere very far away somebody's laughing
and laughing. You are older than you were before.

RADIO TRAFFIC 1: LIPSTICK

Debbie is too much, Maureen divine, & Sue-Anne
an excess of dreamy possibilities. What shall we
do tonight? The High School game is washed out,
but your new perm wasn't meant to be wasted, &
a cracked flask of vodka spills a trickle on the
back seat of Dad's Chev in a message —
Wait for me after the Labomba, near the Gym!
Our needs are plural, we love in duplicate, we
think, as the news bulletin informs us a flash
flood ruins the tennis courts where Bobby lost
her pants & came to grief — Mickey Mouse radios
instruction booklets on golf & polo
neck pullovers cling to the branches as the
mud recedes, yet puppy love is less exciting
when seen through a bottle of hair oil, & crushing
a fresh lemon for a hot drink is more fun
after both the game's best moves & slides
about us playing them expose us to thrilling
insights: illustrated histories of the sexual
habits of tea plantation managers in Malaya delay
our teenage reflexes we can't control & manage
to let us understand how 'wooden' frames
this brilliant landscape in which Latin forms
a new kind of powder, & we swallow it whole. Whoops!
Bobby slipped on the pool tiles where my suntan
lotion spilt & bumped her nipples, yet the soda
diluting a much-needed Campari fails to fizz,
or to solve anything. We share a cigarette, wear
long socks, & go beautifully to either
sleep, or a tennis match delayed by rain.

RADIO TRAFFIC 2: FLAK STATIC

After you cough a tiny spot explodes, then
rain, then heavy weather on the Met Report.
Over Lisbon the Aussie navigator bought it but
the tail gunner's a good kid & finds the way
stockings ladder among a flurry of limbs in
the back seat of an Austin Seven's a sign
of the times, & he's not often wrong.
Though the new navigator got Sparks
confused he soon learned to cope with Spanish
radar & — gulp! Was that a bomb? Isabella!
Where were you when Christopher Columbus
got the pox? A thousand dead Italians make a soup!
But not the soup we need, to wake us up. Below,
Barcelona waits in a hot fog like a bride
eating Laxettes in the dunny, the solution to the
waste problem. How we manage the kiss of death
on the one hand and the flying brothel on the
other's a treat: it's a course in Movie Sucking,
a kind of Tool Shop of the Mind for the 1940s,
& how grimy can you get's the motto in Latin:
ipso facto, a nod is as good as a hangover
in the land of the midnight sun. Drinking
a mug of benzedrine & chocolate over Bremen
might be your idea of suicide, but it's not mine:
a breath of oxygen's timely & revives us
to our duties, & somewhere down there in Europe
a mad genius is planning the atomic bomb. The radio
traffic's hotting up — *Ginger! Are you okay?* His
fingers shaking, the Captain lights a cigarette &
hits the silk. The navigator's dead. Over & out.

RADIO TRAFFIC 3: FOXTROT

A eucalyptus tree has branches & gum leaves
a sticky mark on the footpath, & these are paradigms
for how a tired but happy athlete enters & leaves
follow on a gust of wind: 'Double Exposures' is
a clue but doesn't tell us what he's thinking of.
The Balkans are happy tonight, we hear
a TV star craving a cigarette & a light
goes out all over Europe. On a bronze medal showing
how on a hike into Albania the explorer wears ties
fashion ignored, a new approach to hagiography
is inscribed in Cyrillic script in the
shape of a radio commercial's emblem, &
though we learn it off by heart it fails us
at the very moment we discover
it's a way to understand the shape & form
bad opinions of ourselves. But the shape is elusive &
in the bright glitter that is all that remains
of the explorer's monocle once has has gone for a dip
& lost it in the sand at the bottom of a
mountain stream near the Macedonian coast
we can discern no more than a meniscus at the
edges of a Greek alphabet, & it spells our doom.
If holding an old Kodak's an athletic
exercise snapping the shutter's a
breeze & you soon find a supporting
role in a Jungle Jim movie's a snack.
As you breathe in the gum leaves
move slightly & a blur appears on the film,
so your hopes as an extra take a dive. It's called
'Exploring Bessarabia, Nineteen-ten'.

RADIO TRAFFIC 4: TRICYCLE

Whoops I'm freezing near the 'Manitoba'
no fishing, it's good luck like
finding a nude gipsy under the bed, ah
yes, I'm new to this territory but how
do you say 'ruin' in Italian? The 'Manifesto':
no luck is good luck I'm socially mobile
like popcorn dissolving in the flicker light
from a radioactive movie, & how sweethearts
goof & snicker, trading a quick suck for an Oxford
Credit, is like 'How did they pick up so quick
the enduring habits of the age?' No? It's true,
look, one cigarette & I'm aphasic
near the climax of the traffic jam — wait! —
he's giving her the numbers! Gosh,
he's a ham but he's off the air, he re-named
four of the characters in the Mozart opera
including the loony himself! Yet this is facile,
easy loot, it's 'no chance to sing' & he's
a singer! Ah, yeah, uh, you get the hamburger,
I'll wait here with Louie in the storm, the
lurking storm that deadens the Pacific Ocean —
then the bright weather will return, the automatic
bombers float off to sleep, the pilot sobbing . . .
Look out! That's the 'Manitoba', following us
into the movie theatre, & the Captain fondling
the negro cabin boy — that's not allowed, though
in this our age of sympathy it's possible, it's
possible; bending an ear to the voices whispering
in the radio we hear more than we knew, the
end of a whole age, the glory growing into ruin.

THE WIND

'Due to the shortcomings of indexation etc
all new equipment with technology changes
will be black banned etc' CMX Videotape
Editing NECAM Audio Mixdown wind rushing
up the empty stairwell no one home
Telemation Character Generators Optro-Desk
Digipatch Lighting Systems the telephones
ringing in deserted offices no one at work
hangover holiday 'E.N.G. was introduced . . . without
any prior notification' the traffic buffeted
Digital Delay Slave Units fluorescent lights
fluttering off, floor by floor, 'The best editors
of my generation have resigned for spurious
and often politically-motivated reasons'
in Studio Control the lights are out, only
the glow of the meters and the red, green
and amber push-on push-off buttons on the desk
reflected in the dark glass wall the actors
wandering home through the windy alleys
at the back of William Street 'You have returned
at an inopportune time to an organisation
bereft of any semblance of morale . . .' the light
shudders continuously in the Listening Room
Check Meter Ballistics and Azimuth Malfunction
a Turbo Porsche throttles up the street
knocking down a kid television floats belly up
a balloon of bad dreams the editors have gone
to bed with other people's angry wives
under the scattering wind I look for hints
of a better life

THE GERM

'There's a huge germ behind the glass —
break it, and a terrible plague
will decimate the galaxy!' As he spoke
the Commander grunted agreement. 'You mean
one in ten of us . . . will live?'
'No, die,' came the answer. 'Okay, take a break!'
The director curls up in a corner
and dozes off. He forgot his tablets, and dreams
again about the huge germ eating all his money.
The script girl goes out under the cold stars
for a coffee and a good cry. The glass wall
of the Control Room looks like a mirror,
to the film crew, under the lights; or
history, thinks the sleepy director, the history
we want but never get. 'You making enough money?'
'Sure, sure.' The lights go up, *clack clack*
clack. 'You mean you're in *love* with him?
That bastard?' The script girl's crying again
and the shooting has to stop. These tiny emotions rise
and fall, and many things are changed forever.
'Jim! I can't do it! The Voltage Gate . . . *aaargh!*'
'Listen! You're an alien, aren't you? Well, *try!*'
And yet the history mirror presses against them, and
struggle as they may, the germ is inevitable.
'Nice try, boys! Wrap it up!' They pack up the gear.
'Goodnight!' 'Goodnight!' And far into deep space
in a drifting starship, the aliens turn off the video.
'Some movie, huh?' The crew break out a bottle
but the Commander goes to bed. He has the nightmare
again, about a germ, and a decimated galaxy.

MOONSHINE

I've realised why Ted Berrigan is not so
      hot
            Edward
Berrigan, the Seattle engineer, not
      that other one
He writes to his wife in Kuala Lumpur:
      'What are you up to down there?'
('Doris . . . I'm getting to like middle age . . .')
      See? boring
it's because he has the inborn talents
      of a painter, not an engineer;
no matter how hard he tries, etc.
Another Boeing rolls off the assembly line
      Ted thinks he's okay
he's not okay,
      it's divorce time in Seattle.
He'll be the next to go: Doris! Doris!
      maybe . . .
            Later
imitating the collected works of
      the Darmstadt Engineering Group
reading soup in the darkened kitchen
      he's Canadian, they tell me
an 'emigrant'; his wife's sick
she flies home to Ontario in a Boeing Jumbo —
      did Ted built it? At least the fuselage? She
takes up a fat-free diet; it's goodbye to Seattle,
hello Saskatchewan: middle age
            rises above the tundra
the Boeing plant is bathed in its glow.

'Goodbye Jack Kerouac! We heard you were okay'
    but then you were dead
I think I need an 'ear job'
                                        (it's bad luck
to listen to anything rhyming with 'pig'
like 'Jackson Pollock wore a wig'
                                                      don't listen
your ears go blue and you need a dentist)
'she got up and walked out of the Professor's room'
now why would she do that? you think
she listened to 'Old Snivelly' raving about his
latest archaeological dig
                                        the curse of the dentist
in a movie nightshirt you gape at *Doktor Mabuse*
for the third time, and suddenly realise: it's a
movie, not a talkie! near the banks of the Nile
nobody 'gives a fig' (Shakespeare)
                                                      bang!
                                                              you're deaf
quicker than a typing ribbon
Old 'Spoon-Fed' threw up again
                                                    'goodbye Elvis!'
'is he sick or something?' teeth
connected to the ear bone, etc., in a
thermal, and Mike ripped out the control stick —
'Are you goys okay in there?' movie blather
                                                                    we're okay,
just a little deaf: 'too much
                                            hokey pokey
                                                              down here'

THE GREAT ARTIST RECONSIDERS THE HOMERIC SIMILE

He looks back over the last metaphor
and his eyes shift their focus, his gaze weakly
taking in the litter on the desk and then
the blurred garden, its order and composition:
bare trees, a path strewn with leaves,
a distant figure dawdling at the gate —
light dazzles the window-pane with brilliant
diamonds of dew — he sighs, and drops his pen.
As when a detective in the spring has found
a junk-struck hippy crouching in her pad
at the dead end of Desolation Alley, and
has faked the evidence and booked her, soon
her man returning giftless from his rounds
sees the flat empty and his girl-friend gone;
at that he freaks out, and checks his stride
and with short uneasy steps circles the block,
with smothered groans repeating her name; but she
lies on the cell floor, overdosed,
a heap of bright rags — never again
will those disco mirrors catch her image
floating by, nor the bathroom echo her
withdrawal screams — as that poor addict
hides in horror till the heat cools off,
nor knows his loss, so Matthew Arnold brooded
on his failing similes. His cup of tea
grew cold as he stared out at the Autumn
leaves; a change of air was what he needed,
a holiday at Dover, or Torquay . . .
and as he mused, the lounger at the gate —
the Future — turned his back, and walked away.

See 'Sohrab and Rustum', lines 556-75

A JACKEROO IN KENSINGTON

With a fistful of dollars in a knapsack
and a brutal turn of phrase, colonials
are crashing the party. *Cette parade sauvage:*
on the skyline you can see Rupert Murdoch
crawling over Fleet Street, a pigmy King Kong —
did they shrug off an empire for this?
Too right boss, that's what I want to hear,
the glib, slangy lingo of the tango dancers
steaming through the Heads in a sepia haze —
it's the bottom of the world
say the blond sophisticates. Hang on:
wasn't 'King Kong' invented in America?
The eyes that look into Australia
are European eyes, Peter Porter said, but
my friends' kids holidayed in Hollywood,
and live in San Francisco. I'm
middle-aged, and England made me, cobber,
reading Maugham in the shower recess — though
what about Malraux? and Lao Tzu?
I'm going to be a Chinaman
next time around, speaking perfect English
or Creole, who can choose between
the torrid charms of the one and the
cool, pragmatic bite of the other?
Can you say *You fuckwit!* in Italian?
No way, but if you play Wagner
loud enough you'll get rich quick
in the Bloomsbury sense of the word —
a humus of culture, a knack for sleeping in,
these things adorn you like a froth
and the National Gallery opens its doors
for you, and you alone, at last.

SPEAKEASY

We've checked out the story and it's true —
he was once an overweight philosopher
dizzy with food and fond of spankings,
then he got tanned and rich, in that order,
then he entered politics, and made a killing.
Like a painted model of a car he spoke fluently
but his promises writhed under a net.
What he said became a mass market,
his words are diagrams of sickness
buried in pornography and power graphs,
and he thinks in sub-titles no one
can read fast enough. Don't think his tears
are makeup, they come from a wrecked future
that ends in a million years of darkness,
like yours and mine. His dreams,
at their worst, are not made of images
but a kind of verbal damage. Is he the Poet
we keep asking for, or the one we keep feeding?
Or the one we need? Make it easy,
he begged us, make it easy for me,
idealism is a language I understand,
offer me a deal. My lips are sealed,
he said, then he told us everything.

THE POET AT DURAL

The famous poet phones the famous painter
and a girl's voice answers: Dad? Are you kidding?
Dad's gone to shoot some shit at Dural
with Jack Blank the radio celebrity
a realist and a fan of Ayn Rand,
kicking up trouble on the farm
on the hot line; he can't believe this,
he thought he'd seen everything, but
No! the girl replies, it's true,
they're laughing, they're making deals;
they're in, you're out, you're
old, you're all old, you juice freaks
get old and boring at the speed of light,
this is not a wet dream this is not fantasy
this is your future at the bottom of a glass,
Mum tried to break in but the guard dogs disagreed . . .
the two-way radio the CB star and the
Great Romantic Painter in a time-warp
making the break at Dural: is this a dream?
is this a vision of success gone mad?
The girl is fifteen, the girl says
come around when you sober up, darling,
Dad's at the Palace of Plutus eating
money, you're a boring drunk, go home,
drink up the scotch and drive to Dural,
stand at the gate and read the
latest epic rave to the killer dogs.

THE WATER

The waves do their work patiently
under that large, pallid sky
they take and break into colours,
working at the stones, rehearsing
an endless moronic argument.
The stones are knocked into logical piles
to satisfy the water, and speak no tongue
known to man. Lay your grief down
in a heap, beside the frayed
blue plastic rope, the rusty knife,
and the fish head looking at you.
There's a patch of sand, a baby beach
fringed with ragged grass, and the kids
will stop off there after the barbecue,
get blind drunk, and fuck for hours.
Then they'll sleep, the four of them,
and wake before dawn in a pool of darkness
with gritty cunts, and cocks red raw.
They'll finish the rum, and one will vomit.

Look at these children walking
back slowly, huddled together in couples,
frightened by something like a hangover
but less easily understood: an emotion
attaching itself to their bodies and growing.
The sun rising like a deft simile
plates their hair with fine gold, also
the empty bottle and the puddle of vomit,
the wet rocks, the deceitful speech of the water,
all of it, gleaming, forever.

METEOROLOGY

I fall asleep, alone again, and
passages of music drag me down
then throw me up to the surface
gasping for a cigarette,
and a wonderful man walks in —
the door's open — the heavy weather
turning quickly so I'm caught off-guard:
the sky's his accomplice in these
matters of the heart, or groin,
and in the sunlight a pattern, a satisfying
pattern snaps into focus.
I'm a young woman, aching with the hunger
that makes girls my age
sad, intense and fatal,
and he's been through it all, and shows it,
but I like them mature, don't I? Well,
he's terrific, and we rush off to the beach,
where I get burnt, and that's the pattern,
the bad music reminds me:
no fun without burning, but I like the heat,
and so does he. Then the weather
shifts again, a cold change moves in,
and I'm older when I wake at last.
My lover with the sweet-tasting skin,
why aren't you holding me when I
wake in the early light?

REVERSAL PROCESS

1

I think the instructor's pointing
at you, darling, asking 'Who invented
the perfect colour process?' On the moon
space invaders, back home it's speed reading –
moonlight in a Chev convertible at ninety
and the pages flapping, bright pictures,
the fully-saturated colours are a meal
reading 'Lesbians: A Luxury Moonlight Cruise',
'Flashing Blue Lights in the War Room' or
'Sex and Central Heating – Hidden Dangers.'
At Bondi the beach is freezing and the girls
are mandied, depressed and overweight,
fumbling for sex and money in the Fun Arcade.

2

Lift-off: now the computer tells you the time
like an aphasic baby, its purple numerals
skidding across your eyes. You want to be car-sick
but you're too busy, wow, another heroine,
did all this happen just for you? That
plausible scenery, the light metered perfectly,
those people moving like giraffes, just for you?
The graph paper says it's all external:
'it has existed forever, independent of meaning'
but you know that's bullshit: '*Photo,
ergo sum*' and you can feel the girl's
moist little hand, it's meant for you,
isn't it? The huge harbour glittering
with coloured lights, the way the Leica
looks up at you and just asks to be used,

the way the young girl looks up at you
and slips off her wet bikini, blah, blah,
the two-step, the headache, the pain in the neck,
the bike skidding on the tarmac, the hospital
lit up like a vast mausoleum, it's irresistible —
the illustrations stammering at you
reading: Go, lady, get it while you can.

THE LETTER

Susan thought that she'd forgotten
those shameful things. It must be
twenty years since that girl's body
writhed under Susan's touch,
her young body, firm and scented . . .
memories like that are better buried.
Then this aerogramme from Tucson,
littered with her awkward scrawl:
now, it seems, she's thirty-eight, wrecked
in some American kitchen,
worried about the children, overweight.
A pay packet is torn up,
tears ravage her face,
things have gone from bad to worse,
says her pathetic letter. *Susan,*
write to me, I'm so unhappy. Serve her right.
Susan pours another glass of wine
and tries to read a book, but nothing works:
the rain scribbles its misery across the window,
a heap of leaves is scattered on the lawn.
Maybe her memory lies, perhaps
the girl was plain and commonplace.
Judging from her letter, she's a fool.
There were nasty things, too:
haggling over money, other women,
horrible fights. It lasted one season,
through winter rain, and ended badly.
But her limbs, moving on the bed
in the warm glow of the lamp, her kisses,
her body bucking uncontrollably
and the way she cried out . . . ah, so long ago.
Twenty years — you can't blame her for crying:
it's raining, she's forty, she's alone.

3-D

When you look out the window at the neighbours
then glance back quickly, she seems fine.
Gaunt, maybe, a little neurotic . . .
it's the food she's eating, and the 'happy pills'.
There she goes, listening to important things:
the song bones, the engine wrapped in plastic,
custom pillars supporting a landscape, a jet
ploughing into the mountainside . . . Look
away again, out of the diary. Guess what?
She got a new job, she hated everything. Why
'everything'? Better — better for all of us —
if she could be looked after . . . a luggage locker,
that would be fine, or a holiday resort,
she could shout if she wanted to, couldn't she?
You look away, into the passenger compartment
of the car, and there she is, half alive,
reading the Discovery Kit, over and over.

AT THE CRITERION

I don't go to the pub much any more —
they pulled down the Newcastle ten years ago,
and the Forest Lodge is full of young punks
who can't hold their drink. But now and then —
say, some Friday night when my room
gets on my nerves, with its endless books,
with the pool of lamplight on the table,
the traffic outside my window,
the crowds, the rush and babble, then,
just for old times' sake, I go out.
And she's sure to be there, in the corner bar,
laughing with that young executive
who goes down to the snow in the winter
and has a town house in Double Bay.
They look happy enough. He seems
quite at ease and familiar with her,
though he's only known her a few months —
does he know yet, for example,
that she had an abortion two years ago,
at seventeen, and still isn't over it?
That her mother won't speak to her now
because of the 'immoral things' she did
with her pretty room-mate at College;
that she likes Seafood Avocado, and can't stand
cats, or poverty; and when she makes love
with that awkward desperation, sad and hurried —
at that peak of moaning frenzy
brief tears gather in her eyes: she's not crying,
not happy, just 'a bit out of it', as she says.
Well, he'll learn these things, if he's
attentive, and if it lasts long enough.

Even now — and I'm only on my seventh drink —
she's paying rather too much attention to that
academic type near the door — an older man,
good-looking in a rough sort of way;
a drunk, but with a charming line of talk.
And she prefers older men.
When I've had enough
I'll go back to the flat and pour a scotch
and read over my notes on Cavafy —
a Greek poet, dead long ago,
who lived very fast when he was young
then spent a lonely middle age remembering
his youth in Alexandria, the sordid affairs . . .
patiently sketching a portrait of his
beautiful, corrupt and much-loved city —
'its fever, its absolute devotion to pleasure.'

THE POPULAR MYSTERIES

A fact is as real as
you make it, and your complex
dreaming is a gift factory

as silly as a lucky dip, as
basic as a traffic accident.
And after a quick lunch on the harbour,
a drink picks you up and you
drift off the surface of the planet
daft, adolescent and deeply wise:

a fine glow lights up
your lazy limbs and the nerves
drop away. Behind the blue horizon
a boat disappears, popular mysteries
begin. Your lips fade. You're
asleep, and thoroughly happy.